When Your Goals Seem Out of Reach

Take a Lesson from Nehemiah

GENE A. GETZ

Regal Books

A Division of GL Publications
Ventura, California, U.S.A.

Published by Regal Books
A Division of GL Publications
Ventura, California 93006
Printed in U.S.A.

Library of Congress Cataloging-in-Publication Data.

Getz, Gene A.
   When your goals seem out of reach.

   Previously published as: Nehemiah. © 1981.
   Includes bibliographical references.
   1. Nehemiah (Governor of Judah) 2. Bible. O.T. Nehemiah—Criticism,
interpretation, etc. I. Title.
BS580.N45G47   1987   222'.806   87-12791
ISBN 0-8307-1141-4

Rights for publishing this book in other languages are contracted by Gospel
Literature International (GLINT) foundation. GLINT also provides technical
help for the adaptation, translation, and publishing of Bible study resources
and books in scores of languages worldwide. For further information, contact
GLINT, Post Office Box 488, Rosemead, California, 91770, U.S.A., or the
publisher.

Contents

Acknowledgment

I want to thank Dr. John F. Walvoord, president of Dallas Theological Seminary, for taking time to read this manuscript before it was published in order to evaluate its content. Dr. Walvoord has offered significant encouragement to me personally relative to my written ministry, both in modeling the process in his life as well as giving me positive feedback regarding other published manuscripts.

Renewal:
A Biblical Perspective

Renewal is the essence of dynamic Christianity and the basis on which Christians, both in a corporate or "body" sense and as individual believers, can determine the will of God. Paul made this clear when he wrote to the Roman Christians—"be transformed by the *renewing of your mind.* Then," he continued, "you will be able to test and approve what God's will is" (Rom. 12:2). Here Paul is talking about renewal in both a personal and a corporate sense. In other words, Paul is asking these Christians as a *body* of believers to develop the mind of Christ through corporate renewal.

Personal renewal will not happen as God intended it unless it happens in the context of corporate renewal. On the other hand, corporate renewal will not happen as God intended without personal renewal. Both are necessary.

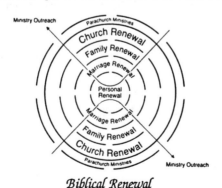

Biblical Renewal

The larger circle represents "church renewal." This is the most comprehensive concept in the New Testament. However, every local church is made up of smaller self-contained, but interrelated units. The *family* in Scripture emerges as the "church in miniature." In turn, the family is made up of an even smaller social unit—*marriage*. The third inner circle represents *personal* renewal, which is inseparably linked to all of the other basic units. Marriage is made up of two separate individuals who become one. The family is made up of parents and children who are also to reflect the mind of Christ. And the church is made up of not only individual Christians, but couples and families.

Though all of these social units are interrelated, biblical renewal can begin within any specific social unit. But wherever it begins—in the church, families, marriages or individuals—the process immediately touches all the other social units. And one thing is certain! All that God says is consistent and harmonious. He does not have one set of principles for the Church and another set for the family, another for husbands and wives, and another for individual Christians. For example, the principles God outlines for local church elders, fathers and husbands, regarding their role as leaders, are interrelated and consistent. If they are not, we can be sure that we have not interpreted God's plan accurately.

The Biblical Renewal Series is an expanding library of books by Gene Getz designed to provide supportive help in moving toward renewal. Each of these books fits into one of the circles described above and will provoke thought, provide interaction and tangible steps toward growth. You will find a detailed listing of the Biblical Renewal Series titles at the back of this book.

Introduction
You Will Identify with Nehemiah

Nehemiah's life and ministry is *not* just a study in leadership. It certainly is that, for he is one of the greatest leaders in the Bible. The management principles that flow from his life to ours are profound and intensely practical. But his approach to problem-solving also illustrates numerous lessons that will help *every* Christian to be a more effective follower of Jesus Christ. Nehemiah's experiences touch us all, particularly as we face the more difficult challenges in life. For example, he models for us:

• How to pray when there seems to be no human solution to our problems.

• How to blend human and divine factors when facing these predicaments.

• How to keep God's sovereignty and our human responsibility in proper balance.

- How to "plan our work" and "work our plan" and at the same time rely on God as our divine resource Person.
- How to handle discouragement in ourselves and others.
- How to set goals and achieve them when everything around us seems to be thwarting our efforts.
- How to motivate others when morale is rapidly deteriorating.
- How to cope with personal anger and other negative emotions.
- How to accept promotion and success without abusing or misusing our privileges.
- How to respond to those who make false accusations against us and malign our motives.
- How to help others develop God's perspective on life.
- How to face and solve the toughest problems in our own lives first.

Every Christian can identify with these practical problems. And Nehemiah encountered them all. Though most of us will never have to face them to the same degree as this Old Testament personality, we will at some time experience the same spiritual and emotional struggles. Even "little" problems seem big at the psychological level. And Nehemiah's perspective on prayer and persistence will help us all to face life's challenges and emerge victorious. Indeed, we "can do all things through Him who strengthens" us (Phil. 4:13).

Welcome to another exciting Old Testament character study!

1

Nehemiah's
Perspective on Prayer

Nehemiah 1:1-11

There are some individuals who have a *special* place in God's scheme of things—people God uses in unique ways to achieve His purposes on earth. Nehemiah was one of those special people. Though his life story does not occupy the same amount of space as some of the other Old Testament individuals God chose to lead the children of Israel, Nehemiah certainly rises tall on the pages of the Old Testament as a dynamic spiritual leader. In fact, we can learn more about this man's specific leadership qualities and skills than we can about any other character in the whole Bible.

We know nothing about Nehemiah's childhood or youth; in fact, we really know very little about his family background. That in itself is unique in biblical history. He was an adult, standing ready to be used to achieve His purposes.

We *do* know that Nehemiah's father's name was Hacaliah (see Neh. 1:1), and his grandparents were probably taken into captivity when Jerusalem fell to the Babylonians. Nehemiah was no doubt born during the exile period.

Gaining Perspective

For years, Israel as a nation existed under the leadership of kings—first of King Saul, followed by David, then by David's son, Solomon. God had promised Israel that if they obeyed Him, He would bless them as a nation. If they did not, then He would curse them and scatter them to the ends of the earth (see Deut. 28:1-68). That promise was repeated to Solomon with a specific application to his own life. If he, as king of Israel, obeyed the Lord he would experience God's continual blessing. If he did not, God warned Solomon He would take away his power and position as king of all Israel (see 1 Kings 9:1-7).

The Divided Kingdom

As happened so frequently among many of Israel's leaders, a good beginning had an unfortunate ending. Solomon sinned against God, particularly by taking unto himself many foreign wives. Eventually he worshiped their false gods. Consequently God dethroned Solomon and, at this juncture in Israel's history, the kingdom was split. The northern tribes were initially ruled by Jeroboam and the southern tribes (Judah and Benjamin) were ruled by Rehoboam (see fig. 1).

The Dispersion

Both kingdoms, however, continued to be characterized by idolatry and immorality. And as God had forewarned, His hand of judgment fell upon all Israel because

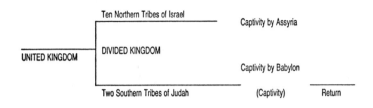

Figure 1
The Divided Kingdom

of their sin. The Northern Kingdom fell first and the people were taken into captivity by the Assyrians. The Southern Kingdom followed suit many years later, and the people were deported by the Babylonians.

The children of Israel who made up the Northern Kingdom were absorbed into the various cultures and communities of the world. However, the people of the Southern Kingdom remained intact and, approximately 70 years later, after the power of Babylon was broken by the Medes and Persians, many began to return to the land of Canaan.

The Return Under Zerubbabel

In approximately 536 B.C. the first group returned to Judah under the leadership of Zerubbabel (fig. 2; see Ezra 1—6). Over a period of years and amidst tremendous opposition from the Samaritans, they eventually succeeded in rebuilding the Temple.

The Return Under Ezra

A number of years later—about 458 B.C.—a second group of Jews returned, led by Ezra (see Ezra 7:1-10). Arriving on the scene, they found the children of Israel in a state of spiritual and moral degradation. They had inter-

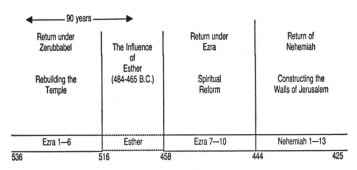

Figure 2
Panorama of Ezra-Nehemiah

married with the unbelieving peoples of the surrounding nations and were participating in their pagan practices. However, through Ezra's faithful teaching ministry, the majority of these people turned from their sins and once again followed God's will for their lives (see fig. 2). These events all set the stage for Nehemiah's appearance in Old Testament history.

The Return of Nehemiah

Several years following Ezra's return to Jerusalem, Nehemiah also returned and God used him to guide Israel in rebuilding the walls of the city and in reordering their social and economic life (see fig. 2). What he was able to accomplish in a brief period of time was an incredible feat. How he accomplished this goal is one of the major emphases of this book. As we observe his leadership skills, as well as his total life-style, we, as twentieth-century Christians, can glean supracultural principles that will help all of us function more productively as members of God's family.

The Problem in Jerusalem

As stated earlier, Nehemiah suddenly appears in the Old Testament as a grown and responsible adult. Though in captivity, he had risen to a position of respect and prominence in his pagan environment. He was serving King Artaxerxes as his personal cupbearer (see 1:11; 2:1).

This important position in the king's court in itself gives us some very helpful insights into Nehemiah's life and character. A mighty monarch like the king of Persia would only select a man for this position who was very wise, who had demonstrated unlimited discretion, and who was totally honest and trustworthy. In addition to testing the king's wine and guarding his sleeping quarters (to make sure he was not assassinated), Nehemiah was probably consulted often for advice and counsel by the king himself. In other words, Nehemiah's position alone reveals volumes regarding this man's intellectual capabilities, his emotional maturity and his spiritual status.

Hanani's Depressing Report (Neh. 1:1-3)

While serving as the king's cupbearer at the main palace in Susa, Nehemiah one day received a report from several men who had come from Jerusalem. One of these men was his own brother, Hanani. This report, which was destined to dramatically interrupt Nehemiah's regular work routine, came "in the month Chislev" (1:1)—which would overlap our months of November and December.

The report was prompted by a question from Nehemiah, which also tells us something about this man. In the midst of his own life of relative ease and luxury, Nehemiah was concerned about what was happening to his own people who had returned to Jerusalem. "What about my brothers?" he asked. "How are they? And what is Jerusalem like?" (see 1:2).

Nehemiah was instantly depressed by what he heard. "The remnant there in the province who survived the captivity are in great distress and reproach," they replied. "And the wall of Jerusalem is broken down and its gates are burned with fire" (1:3).

Nehemiah's Initial Response (Neh. 1:4)

Knowing what we already know about Nehemiah's character, we can somewhat predict his response to the report from Jerusalem. But only the specific words in Scripture reveal the depth of this man's concern and sensitivity for his own people. He "sat down and *wept* and *mourned* for days,"[1] Exactly how long this was we do not know. But it does say *"for days."* And as we'll see in our next chapter, it could have been as long as four months! He was so involved emotionally that he would not eat—at least on a regular basis—but spent the time in prayer for his fellow Jews in Jerusalem (see 1:4).

This is indeed significant behavior for a man who had access regularly to the king's kitchen and the most exquisite food and drink in the land. How easy it would have been for Nehemiah to avoid the Jerusalem problem! How tempting to lose himself in his own fortunate situation! How convenient to not even ask the question! After all, what could he do about the plight of his fellow Jews!

But this was not Nehemiah's attitude nor his response. His own comfortable existence only accentuated his concern for the children of Israel—another reflection of Nehemiah's sterling character.

Nehemiah's Specific Prayer

There are times when God led scriptural writers to elaborate on certain concepts to achieve certain special goals. We have a graphic illustration of that process in Nehemiah's prayer. Earlier we read in one simple statement that Nehemiah was "praying" (1:4) about the disheartening situation in Jerusalem. In the next seven verses—the rest of chapter 1—we are told *how* he prayed and *what* he prayed. Inherent in this process is perhaps one of the greatest lessons we can learn from his life. This is why I believe the Holy Spirit led Nehemiah to record in detail the content of his prayer.

He acknowledged God's greatness. Nehemiah faced a situation he knew he could not solve by himself. From a human point of view it was impossible. But he also knew that God is not characterized by human limitations. With Him *all* things are possible because of who He is! Nehemiah began his prayer by acknowledging that fact: "I beseech Thee, O Lord [Yahweh] God of heaven, the *great* and awesome God . . . " (1:5).

With this statement Nehemiah recognized God's unfathomable greatness—His power, His all-knowing qualities, His omnipresence and His majesty. And Nehemiah also acknowledged that God never forgets His promises. This is evident by the fact that he used the divine name *Yahweh*—a title the children of Israel used of God when they referred to His covenant relationship with them. And Nehemiah's next statement to Yahweh demonstrates specifically why he used this name for God.

He reminded God of His covenant with Israel. "I beseech Thee, O Lord [Yahweh] . . . who preserves *the covenant* . . ." (1:5). And a few verses later Nehemiah became even more *specific* in reminding God of His promises to Israel: "Remember the word which Thou didst command Thy servant Moses, saying, 'If you are unfaithful I will *scatter you* . . . ; but if you return to Me . . . I will *gather them*' " (1:8,9).

It may seem strange that Nehemiah reminded an all-knowing God of His promises. Did not God remember? Of course He did! He was and is omniscient. But it pleased Him to hear one of His faithful children review His promises in His presence. It certainly indicated that not all of His chosen people had forsaken His will and His ways. Remember, to disobey God also means to forsake God Himself. And this is what had happened to most of the people in Israel. That, of course, explains why Nehemiah's prayer next dealt with Israel's sin.

He confessed Israel's sin. "*We* have sinned against

Thee" Nehemiah prayed. "*We* have acted very corruptly against Thee and have not kept the commandments, nor the statutes, nor the ordinances which Thou didst command Thy servant Moses" (1:6,7).

Notice that Nehemiah included himself in this prayer. In fact, he was very specific, "*I* and my father's house have sinned" (1:6). Like Daniel the prophet, he also bore the responsibility for Israel's disobedience (see Dan. 9:4-6). Though both Nehemiah and Daniel no doubt remained true to God during the captivity—at least more so than many in Israel—they did not rationalize away their involvement in Israel's corporate failure as a nation. Consequently, they confessed Israel's corporate sin, and included themselves.

But Nehemiah also reminded God that some in Israel (including himself) still acknowledged who He was and desired to obey Him. They had *not* bowed down to false gods. Therefore, he prayed, "O Lord, I beseech Thee, may Thine ear be attentive to the prayer of *Thy servant* and the prayer of *Thy servants who delight to revere Thy name*" (Neh. 1:11). And at this point, he made his request very specific.

He asked God for personal help. Humanly speaking, there was only one individual who could make it possible for Nehemiah to help the Jews in Jerusalem—the king whom he served. That is why Nehemiah prayed very specifically, "Make Thy servant successful today, and grant him compassion before this man [that is King Artaxerxes]" (1:11).

Nehemiah's specific request again reflects his character. Not only was he willing to approach God and pray for his people, but he was also willing to be the channel through whom God could work to solve this problem.

This was no simple decision. Nehemiah was not naive. He knew what lay ahead of him should he leave the king's court and go to Jerusalem. Not only would he give up a choice position with security and safety, but his very life was at stake—and indeed it proved to be so, as we'll see in future chapters. But Nehemiah was a man who loved God *and* his people. And come what may, he was willing to pay the price.

Nehemiah's Prayer Process and the Twentieth-Century Christian

There are many lessons that emerge from Nehemiah's experience as it is recorded in the first chapter of the book that bears his name. His integrity, concern, and compassion are exemplary. But no quality stands out more graphically than his belief that "the effective prayer of a righteous man can accomplish much" (Jas. 5:16). And prayer was not something Nehemiah simply talked about. He prayed! He demonstrated with his life the effectiveness of our communicating with God our deepest needs—particularly in times of crisis, difficulty, and tribulation. It is in these moments of pain and helplessness that we need to remember that we have access to the One who can help us make our way through life's periods of deep difficulty.

What makes Nehemiah's example of prayer so unique in this instance is what we can learn from his own experience in prayer. He outlines for us, with his own approach to prayer, a process that we can apply in our own periods of crisis.

But before we apply the actual *content* of his prayer to our own lives, let's look first at his attitudes and actions that accompanied his prayer for help.

Our Conduct in Prayer

*God honors prayer expressed out of a heart of **deep concern**.* Nehemiah voiced his prayer to God out of a heart deeply moved with compassion for the suffering Jews in Jerusalem. And when any one of God's children approaches His throne with deep concern, the Lord's heart is touched. Jesus dramatically illustrated this fact with the parable of the unrighteous judge and the poor widow. Though the judge was a man who did "not fear God" or "respect man" (Luke 18:4), he responded to this woman's request for help. Jesus applied the lesson in the story by reminding us that God, who is a *righteous* judge, will "bring about justice for His elect, who cry to Him day and night" (Luke 18:7). God *does* honor prayer expressed out of a heart of concern.

*God honors prayer that takes **priority** over other needs.* The Bible speaks rather frequently of fasting, and this experience is often associated with prayer. The purpose of fasting is not to abstain from food per se, but to allow us to spend the time in prayer which we would ordinarily spend eating. The apostle Paul also makes reference to abstaining from sexual relations in marriage on occasions in order to spend time in prayer. In fact, he implies that this is the *only* reason to abstain from this marital responsibility (see 1 Cor. 7:5).

In both of these examples, God is teaching us that there are times when we should abstain from meeting our physical and emotional needs in order to spend time communicating with Him about more important concerns and needs. And when we do, God's heart is touched in a special way. It demonstrates to Him our sincerity and our willingness to sacrifice our own desires in order to get His attention. It is a true test of our motives. And as we have seen, this was certainly verified in Nehemiah's experience, for he fasted and prayed for many days about Israel's predicament in Jerusalem.

*God honors **persistent** prayer.* Jesus confirmed this truth in His parable we referred to earlier. The poor widow is heard by the unrighteous judge because "she *kept coming* to him" with her request (Luke 18:3). The application is clear. If a wealthy man of the world who could care less about the deep needs of a poor widow woman responded to her *persistence,* how much more will God—who cares about our every need—respond when we "cry to Him day and night" (Luke 18:7; see also Matt. 6:25,26). Nehemiah experienced this truth as he sought God's help for Israel. God indeed honors persistent prayer!

Our Content in Prayer

Like Nehemiah, we must recognize God's greatness. He is a holy God and the sovereign Lord of the universe. We must approach Him with reverence and awe. Jesus illustrated this truth with the model prayer He shared with His followers. "Pray, then, in this way: 'Our Father who art in heaven, *hallowed be Thy name*'" (Matt. 6:9).

Though God is our friend, we must not take that friendship for granted. He is still God and we are but human beings. We must constantly recognize the One we are talking to.

Like Nehemiah, we can also remind God of His promises to us. Though He is great and awesome, He is approachable and He desires that we come to Him in prayer.

Why would God want us to remind Him—the omniscient One—of what He has promised? Doesn't He remember what He has said? Of course He does. The fact that we verbalize to God what He has promised indicates to Him that we actually *know* and *believe* what He has said. Though it is difficult for us to understand this point, He enjoys and appreciates being heard.

Think for a moment what happens to a teacher who gives an exam to his students and they accurately verbalize back what he has spent hours communicating. He loves and appreciates it. And that teacher feels even *more* love and appreciation when the students *act* upon what they have learned. The point is clear! Though God is no ordinary teacher, He does respond positively to those who act on what he has taught them.

Like Nehemiah, we must acknowledge our unworthiness and sinfulness, our human weaknesses and failings, as we approach God. We must remember we have a unique advantage, even Nehemiah. Jesus Christ has died for us and the apostle John reminds us that "if we walk in the light as He Himself is in the light, we have fellowship with one another, and the blood of Jesus His Son cleanses us from all sin" (1 John 1:7). Further, John says, "If we confess our sins, He is faithful and righteous to forgive us our sins and to cleanse us from all unrighteousness" (1:9).

Actually, John is telling us that Christ's blood *keeps on cleansing* us from all sin. We are already forgiven in Christ if we have accepted in our hearts His personal sacrifice for us; but we must constantly walk in the light, acknowledging our continuing sinfulness. As we do, God responds to our prayers.

Like Nehemiah, we must be specific in our prayers in order to get specific answers. Paul exhorted the Philippians, "Be anxious for nothing, but *in everything* by prayer and supplication with thanksgiving let your requests be made known to God" (Phil. 4:6). There is nothing so small that God is not interested in it. And there is nothing so big that He cannot help us with it. We must not hesitate to be *specific* in our requests.

A Twentieth-Century Miracle

Let me illustrate how Nehemiah's process affected my own life and a number of other Christians in a dramatic way. For nearly a year and a half I helped start a branch church in the Park Cities area of Dallas. A group of us in the home base church (Fellowship Bible Church in North Dallas) were confident that God wanted a new church in what was the most exclusive area of the city. We soon discovered, however, what seemed to be an impossible situation. Property values were out of sight. And the property that was available was very scarce and involved small plots that were not large enough for a church. The fact is that a church building had not been constructed in that part of Dallas for nearly 25 years.

We looked and prayed for months—in the meantime meeting on Sunday evenings in a rented facility, paying an exorbitant fee.

Many of us were getting very discouraged. Though God was meeting our needs, the situation seemed hopeless on a long-range basis. We had already learned from other experiences in starting branch churches that without a permanent facility, it is difficult in our culture to have a successful ministry. Would we be able to make the new church succeed?

In the meantime, I became impressed with Nehemiah's process in prayer as he faced what appeared to be an impossible task. I could identify with his helpless feelings in being able to do anything to resolve the problem he faced. I even sensed some of the helplessness that our people were beginning to feel and wondered how long they would be willing to participate in a ministry that seemed to be faltering because of our rather dead-end search.

One evening I shared with the church body the lessons I've just enumerated from Nehemiah's prayer process. And at that moment the Lord seemed to give me faith to believe that Nehemiah's approach to prayer would also work for us. In fact, in retrospect, I sometimes am tempted to wonder if I was not being a bit presumptuous. But, after sharing Nehemiah's experience, I then led the church body through the same steps taken by this Old Testament leader.

1. *With the use of Scripture, hymns, and prayer, we acknowledged God's greatness!* We let Him know that we knew and believed that He could find us a piece of property and/or a permanent facility, even though it seemed to be a

human impossibility. If He could resolve Nehemiah's predicament, we told Him we believed He could solve ours.

2. *We reminded God of His promises to us.* Various members of the body openly shared scriptural statements with the Lord. Among those shared were Jesus' words recorded by Matthew in his Gospel, "Ask, and it shall be given to you; seek, and you shall find; knock, and it shall be open to you. For every one who asks receives; and he who seeks finds; and to him who knocks it shall be opened" (Matt. 7:7,8).

3. *We confessed our sins to God.* Individually and as a body we claimed forgiveness which we have in Jesus Christ.

4. *We were very specific in our prayers.* We asked God to lead us to people who could help us—both Christians and non-Christians. If God could use Artaxerxes, we believed there were people in Dallas who could help us if God moved on their hearts and gave us opportunity to make our needs known. We asked for miraculous resources financially, for ours were very limited. We hardly had enough income to pay the rent on our facility and some part-time salaries. In short, we were praying for a miracle! And indeed it would take a miracle, for we felt at that moment that we had exhausted every human resource.

What happened *was* a miracle! God answered in ways we could not have contrived. I'll share that answer very specifically in the next chapter, for it correlates dramatically with Nehemiah's experience.

Life Response

Select a need, whether large or small, and apply the prayer lessons from Nehemiah's life. Use the following both as a checklist and a guideline for your prayer process.

NOTE: These steps can be used in your personal prayer life or with a group.

Heart Attitude
1. ☐ I am deeply concerned about this matter.
2. ☐ I am willing to forego meeting other needs to spend time in prayer.
3. ☐ I am going to be persistent in prayer.

Prayer Process
1. ☐ Recognize God's greatness and His awesome power.
2. ☐ Remind God of His promises.
3. ☐ Acknowledge sin and claim forgiveness in Christ.
4. ☐ Be specific in prayer.

Note
1. Hereafter all italicized words in Scripture quotations are added by the author for emphasis.

Nehemiah's
Unique Balance

Nehemiah 2:1-8

What Nehemiah had hoped *would not happen,* but feared *would happen*—actually *happened!* When he discovered that the wall of Jerusalem was "broken down" and its gates were "burned with fire" and that the Jews were in "great distress and reproach," he immediately "sat down and wept and mourned for days." It was as if Nehemiah had expected "bad news," but not that bad. This interpretation of Nehemiah's response is not pure conjecture. Many Bible scholars believe that Artaxerxes—the king he served as cupbearer—had actually issued a decree sometime earlier to thwart the Jews in their efforts to rebuild the wall in Jerusalem. This is clearly described in Ezra 4.[1]

Rehum, a Persian official in Samaria, had written to Artaxerxes and informed him that the Jews he had allowed to return to Jerusalem were rebuilding the city and were actually "finishing the walls and repairing the foundations" (Ezra 4:12). "Let it be known to the king," he reported, "that if that city is rebuilt and the walls are finished, they will not pay tribute, custom, or toll, and it will damage the revenue of the kings" (4:13).

Artaxerxes took the content of this disturbing epistle under advisement. As suggested in the letter, he researched the history of Jerusalem and recognized the

potential threat and danger should the city be rebuilt.
Consequently, he countered with a letter of his own (see
4:17-20), issuing a command to stop the work in Jerusalem. And as soon as Rehum had received the king's
letter, he "went in haste to Jerusalem to the Jews and
stopped them by force of arms" (4:23).

We can only speculate regarding what happened specifically, but it seems rather clear from the report which
Nehemiah received from the men who came from Judah
that the results of Artaxerxes' letter were devastating.
Rehum and his cohorts must have literally attacked the
wall of Jerusalem and broken it down and set fire to the
gates.

Because of Nehemiah's position in the king's court, he
must have been aware of Rehum's initial letter and
Artaxerxes' subsequent response. However, he had probably not received word as to the results of the letter, though
he probably feared for his brothers in Jerusalem. It is with
this prior knowledge that he received the disappointing
report from Jerusalem with a sense of deep regret and
despair.

But there is something even more significant in this
account that can be legitimately read between the lines. It
was against this backdrop that Nehemiah prayed to God to
"grant him compassion before this man" (Neh. 1:11).
Humanly speaking, Artaxerxes was the only person who
could help the Jews. He had issued the order to stop the
building process in the first place; only he could reverse it.
It is no wonder that Nehemiah turned to the only Source
who could help him solve the problem. Only God could
help him change the king's mind and cause him to be
compassionate, both towards Nehemiah and the people he
wanted so desperately to help.

Nehemiah's Unique Opportunity (Neh. 2:1,2)

Four months went by before Nehemiah's opportunity

came—from Chislev (November-December) to Nisan (March-April). Seemingly it happened at a special banquet, since the queen was at Artaxerxes' side (2:6). Nehemiah was going about his usual duties serving wine.

But something was uniquely different about Nehemiah's countenance. Since this was the first time his servant had ever looked dejected in his presence the king sensed it immediately. "Why is your face sad though you are not sick?" the king inquired. And with penetrating insight he continued, "This is nothing but sadness of heart" (2:2).

At that moment Nehemiah was very frightened. And understandably so! For one thing, his job description was very specific. He was *never* to be sad in the king's presence. In fact, *any* subject to the king of Persia was in danger of severe punishment for demonstrating anything but a joyful countenance while on duty.

But more important was the strategic responsibility that lay on Nehemiah's shoulders at this moment. Should the king actually respond favorably to his deep concern, what would he say to the man who issued an earlier order causing the very condition that had broken Nehemiah's spirit?

Nehemiah's Wise Response (Neh. 2:3,4)

It is clear that Nehemiah had been thinking long and hard about this moment he knew would eventually come. Though Artaxerxes' observations frightened him, he was ready with his response. "Let the king live forever," he answered, assuring the king of his personal loyalty. And then, he dealt with the real issue—*but* cautiously. "Why should my face not be sad when the *city,* the place of my *fathers' tombs,* lies desolate and its gates have been consumed by fire?" (2:3).

Nehemiah avoided naming Jerusalem. On the surface this may sound like a simple response. Not so. Note that

Nehemiah did not identify the "city" by name. Though he was not trying to deceive the king, he no doubt wanted to avoid putting Artaxerxes on the defensive, causing an immediate negative reaction. After all, Artaxerxes had previously, and perhaps recently, researched the history of this city—the city of *Jerusalem*—and what he discovered disturbed him so much he had issued an order against the city so it could not be rebuilt and threaten his power and financial resources (see Ezra 4:19,20).

Nehemiah appealed to the king's sense of respect—his sense of "rightness" regarding proper respect for the dead. Since ancestral reverence permeated the Middle Eastern culture, Nehemiah hoped that he might strike a responsive chord in Artaxerxes' heart. Consequently, he answered the king's inquiry about his sadness by reminding him that no individual could be happy when the city and place of his *"father's tombs* lies desolate."

Nehemiah must have waited with bated breath for the king's answer, with questions flooding his mind. Would he be severely punished for losing emotional control in the presence of the king? Would he be transferred to another position, eliminating the only human possibility for helping his brothers in Jerusalem? Would the king even take his situation seriously and pursue the matter further?

In spite of Nehemiah's weakened condition physically and psychologically, the king's response must have sent chills up and down his spine. "What would you request?" asked the king (Neh. 2:4).

At this juncture Nehemiah *knew* God was at work answering prayer. And he also knew at this strategic moment that he desperately needed God's continued help. While in the very process of formulating an answer to Artaxerxes' critical question, he quickly whispered a prayer to God. We don't know the specific content of this rather hurried prayer, but had it been me, I would have certainly needed to ask for both strength in my knees and wisdom to express my thoughts clearly and comprehensively. At a time like this it's easy to go blank and forget everything. Fear does amazing things to the brain. I'm sure Nehemiah faced some of the same trauma.

Nehemiah's Bold Request (Neh. 2:5-8)

As you continue reading this first-person account, it becomes more and more obvious that Nehemiah had done his homework in preparation for this moment he had prayed for—which is one of the most significant lessons that emerges from this brief passage of Scripture. Nehemiah not only prayed and sought God's help, but he utilized all of the human resources available, including his intellectual capabilities, his human experiences, his accumulated wisdom, his role and position in life, and people with whom he came in contact—in this instance, the king of Persia.

Putting it succinctly, Nehemiah carefully and wisely blended both divine and human resources to achieve his goals, a theme that is intricately interwoven into most of the events that are described in this Old Testament story. And when all was said and done, as we'll see in a moment, he ultimately gave all glory and honor to God no matter how much he was able to use his human capabilities and skills. Verses 5-8 illustrate this process at work.

Nehemiah had prayed specifically for an opportunity to win a hearing with Artaxerxes (see 1:4-11) and when that opportunity came, he again sought God's help (see 2:4). This is clear from the way Nehemiah has already answered the king's questions. By not mentioning Jerusalem specifically he avoided putting the king on the defensive. By referring to his "fathers' tombs" he demonstrated awareness of the king's strong reverence for ancestors. Furthermore, we see Nehemiah's preparation for this moment by the way he made his bold request.

Nehemiah asked the king to send him to Judah, the

"city" of his "fathers' tombs" that he might "rebuild it" (2:5). And once again, Nehemiah referred to having proper respect for his ancestors, and once again he avoided naming the city. By now, Artaxerxes certainly knew *what* city he was referring to, but Nehemiah avoided putting pressure on Artaxerxes. Perhaps he was also being sensitive to the king in view of the fact that the queen would certainly be listening in on the conversation (see 2:6). She would have found it easy to remind Artaxerxes of his earlier decision, which would have triggered his male ego and made it much more difficult for him to respond positively to Nehemiah's request. If this be true, we must give Nehemiah even more credit for "word-smithing" his responses to coincide with the queen's presence.

The king then asked Nehemiah when he would return if he gave him permission to go to Jerusalem. Nehemiah responded immediately with a "definite time" (v. 6), again indicating forethought.

No doubt the king responded favorably to Nehemiah's specific answer, for Nehemiah proceeded immediately to ask for the biggest favors yet. When thinking through the whole process ahead of time, he knew that a trip to Jerusalem without the king's special permission and personal resources would fail. There would be little he could do for his brothers. Consequently, he asked two things.

First, he requested letters of permission from the king himself to allow him to pass through the various provinces so he could reach Jerusalem without opposition (see 2:7). How well he must have remembered the letter from Rehum, the governor of Samaria, that requested the king to issue an order to stop the Jews from rebuilding the city. Nehemiah was well aware that the only way he would be permitted to pass through the various provinces was by special permission from the king, for every governor along the way would be resistant to Nehemiah's goals and objectives for Jerusalem.

Second, he asked for a letter to Asaph, the man in charge of the king's forest, so that he could have access to materials to rebuild the walls and other parts of the city (see 2:8). It did not just happen by chance that Nehemiah was aware of the fact that one of the king's forests was near Jerusalem. Even more startling, he actually knew the *name* of the man who was in charge.

Nehemiah had not only prayed persistently that God would "grant him compassion" before the king, but he had worked very hard preparing himself to discuss the issue intelligently and wisely when his opportunity came. Because of this unique blend of human and divine effort, Nehemiah was able to achieve what initially appeared to be an impossible goal.

Nehemiah's Humble Tribute (Neh. 2:8)

The key to Nehemiah's success in this situation is stated clearly in his tribute to God following his successful dialogue with Artaxerxes: "And the king granted them to me *because the good hand of my God was on me*" (2:8). Though Nehemiah had worked diligently preparing himself for the time he would have opportunity to share his burden with the king, and though he was able to demonstrate unusual wisdom in responding to the king's questions, when all was said and done he knew his success was dependent on God's help. As we'll see in future chapters, this quality of life characterized Nehemiah throughout his entire ministry.

Maintaining Balance in Today's World

As Christians we must maintain a proper balance between divine and human factors in doing the will of God on earth. On the one hand Nehemiah had prayed, seeking God's help, realizing it was impossible for him to solve the problem on his own. On the other hand, he applied himself diligently to do all he could to prepare himself for the moment God would open a door to the king's mind and heart.

God's children today must use the same approach if we are going to be effective Christians in our twentieth-century world. This is a major lesson that can be written across the pages of the first eight verses of chapter 2 in the book of Nehemiah.

Peril of the pendulum. As Christians we tend toward two extremes. *First, at times the work of God flounders because we do not do all we can to prepare ourselves for the task ahead of us.* The opportunity comes and passes us by because we are not properly equipped to meet it. In some instances we do not even recognize the opportunity. And if we do, we have neither the knowledge, emotional confidence nor the skills to do what we must in order to be successful.

Our relying on prayer alone is never God's way of achieving His goals on earth. Merely trusting Him as the Sovereign of the universe is a superficial approach theologically. He is indeed sovereign, but He has placed upon all of us significant human responsibility. It is sometimes difficult to balance these two concepts pragmatically, but it is absolutely essential in order to be effective in our ministry for the Lord. This balance is illustrated again and again in the Bible, and Nehemiah is one of the classic examples.

The other extreme is that at times the work of God flounders because we take matters into our own hands. We do not seek God's help. We rely primarily on our own wisdom and skills. We may use the words "prayer" and "faith" but they are merely that—words. They represent the right thing to say, but our behavior demonstrates we are still attempting to solve problems more humanistically than spiritually.

Maintaining this intricate balance is a constant challenge to every Christian. It is almost natural to go to extremes. The peril of the pendulum tempts us regularly.

Answered prayer. The most encouraging lesson in this Old Testament story is that God *does* answer prayer. With Him even the impossible becomes possible.

In chapter 1 I shared with you the beginning of a story. As a small group of Christians in Dallas we faced a "Jerusalem" experience. Our "walls were broken down." Translated into twentieth-century language, we believed God wanted us to establish a church in the Park Cities area of Dallas—a branch of Fellowship Bible Church. Property was scarce, and what was available was priced out of sight. The picture was bleak and discouraging.

We did the only thing we could do. For a year and a half we looked. Yes, we prayed too, but not like Nehemiah. And then we decided to follow his example. We acknowledged God's greatness, reminded Him of His promises, confessed our sins and claimed forgiveness in Christ. Finally, we prayed specifically, asking God to do what seemed to be the impossible. (For a more detailed description of Nehemiah's process and how we applied it in our own situation, see chapter 1—particularly pages 13,14).

The very evening we used Nehemiah's prayer process, a woman was visiting for the first time. I did not know who she was or that she was even there until I received a call from her boss the next day. He wanted to meet with me to talk about our concern. His secretary had shared with him what she had experienced the evening before as she heard my message from Nehemiah chapter 1, and then observed how we had applied Nehemiah's prayer approach to our own predicament. Later he shared with me that his secretary had commented, "Those people really practice true Christianity." I was thrilled of course with this feedback. Obviously this newcomer had sensed our deep concern and faith, though I must admit I was also struggling deep inside with the magnitude of the miracle we were asking God to perform.

My initial meeting with this man led to another meeting with two more of our elders. He volunteered to do everything he could to help us find property. "I know the Park Cities like the back of my hand," he said. "As a kid I used to ride my bicycle up and down these streets."

Together we brainstormed. Some ideas were totally unworkable. But we wanted to explore every possibility. Finally, our new friend asked the chairman of our elder board if he had talked with a certain Christian developer who was building beautiful and expensive homes on the Caruth homestead. The elder had, a year ago, but there was no possibility at that time of obtaining a piece of property for a church.

The Caruth homestead is a large piece of property located in Dallas. Bordering Central Expressway on the east and Northwest Highway to the north, it was at that point one of the major undeveloped sections of land in the main part of the city. To the east and southeast of this property are the Park Cities. To the north is the expansive Northpark Shopping Center, one of the most exquisite of its kind in the world.

Our chairman agreed to contact the developer again. To our surprise—which shows how we often limit God— the developer responded with a tentative yes. He showed us a two-and-a-half-acre plot in the homestead he would consider relinquishing for our church—if the other principals agreed! The price—$275,000. Though this was an enormous sum of money for a small group, it was a very reasonable price for that property which shortly thereafter doubled and tripled in value.

Miraculously, all those involved agreed to sell the property to Fellowship Bible Church of Park Cities. Later the developer reported that if we had contacted him one week earlier or one week later, it probably would have been impossible to secure the property. This added to the miraculous nature of our prayer process and the results.

However, we faced another serious problem. Where would we get $275,000? Sacrificially, our people (fewer than 30 committed family units) were able to get together $75,000 at the most.

And then God worked another miracle. I approached a friend about the property—a friend God had blessed in an unusual way financially, but who did not attend any of our Fellowship churches. However, she believed wholeheartedly in our ministry. "Yes," she said, "I'm interested in helping." She volunteered to pay the interest on the remaining $200,000 for a three-year period. "Furthermore," she said, "I'll sign for an additional loan to build a building."

The miracle was unfolding before our eyes. But my friend's signature was not enough to convince the bank to lend us the total sum of money to build the building, though they realized the great value of the two-and-one-half acres of land.

Then came the next miracle. One of our elders had lived next door and had grown up in the Park Cities with the son of a well-known Dallas businessman. With fear blended with trust he approached this man regarding the possibility of obtaining his signature on a loan. The response? Without hesitation, "Sure, I'll sign." And he did, which clenched the loan.

The days that followed brought more miracles. But all of this began when we prayed, like Nehemiah, with deep concern. Out of our frustration we asked God for help. We prayed specifically. We approached God for the impossible, and he answered. We discovered experientially that God is still the God of Abraham, Isaac and Jacob and of all Israel. And He is our God, too! When we, as a body of believers, pray in unity, when our hearts are right toward

God, and when we pray in accordance with His will, He responds! Fellowship Bible Church of Park Cities located on the Caruth homestead proves it!

Life Response

To what extent are you balancing the divine and the human factors in doing God's work. Are you laying back and waiting for Him to do it all? Or are you trying to do it all yourself?

There is a balance. With God's help you can find it in the varying situations in life. Begin now—today—to commit yourself to finding that balance. The following guidelines will help you:

1. Consult the Word of God regularly.

2. In times of uncertainty and crisis, use Nehemiah's prayer process no matter what your concerns, be they large or small.

3. Seek advice from other mature members of Christ's body.

4. Allow circumstances to influence you but not to discourage you. What may appear to be impossible may indeed be possible with God's help.

5. Interpret your own personal "feelings" about the matter carefully. Remember, the feelings of confidence may be feelings of pride. And feelings of distress may reflect natural reactions under the circumstances.

Remember this! If Nehemiah had followed his feelings, he would have given up!

Note

1. There is a difference of opinion regarding this historical theory. Some Bible interpreters believe that the term "Artaxerxes" was a general title which applied to more than one ruler and in this instance the "Artaxerxes" Nehemiah served as cupbearer was a different man than the one Ezra referred to in chapter four of the book that bears his name. However, others believe that Ezra 4:6-23 is a parenthetical passage and refers to the same Artaxerxes as mentioned in Nehemiah. After carefully considering both views, I have personally accepted the latter view as the most feasible. You will note that I followed this historical hypothesis in explaining the text of Nehemiah.

3

Nehemiah's
Preliminary Preparation

Nehemiah 2:9-20

A university president once said that there are three kinds of people in the world—"Those who don't know what is happening, those who watch what's happening, and those who make things happen."

From a human point of view Nehemiah was a man who *made* things happen. But unlike so many today, when things happened he knew it was not only his human ingenuity and his hard work that caused it but also God's blessing upon him. Thus when the king made it possible for him to go to Jerusalem to rebuild the city, Nehemiah acknowledged without equivocation, "And the king granted them to me *because the good hand of my God was on me*" (Neh. 2:8).

Nehemiah Journeys to Jerusalem (Neh. 2:9,10)

Nehemiah had experienced a marvelous miracle. Though he had worked hard preparing himself for the opportunity that came his way, he understood clearly that it had all transpired because *God's good hand was upon him* (see 2:8). In fact, when he asked the king for permission to go to Jerusalem to rebuild the city, and for official letters to cross over the various borders unhindered, and for a special letter to Asaph to give him access to the king's forest, he actually got more than he had asked for. The king also sent with Nehemiah "officers of the army and horsemen" (2:9) to escort him safely to Jerusalem.

Can you imagine the excitement that must have gripped Nehemiah's heart? After months of praying, mourning and fasting as he faced what seemed to be an impossible situation, he now found himself in the midst of a king's escort headed for Jerusalem with official letters signed and sealed by Artaxerxes himself. This *was* a miracle.

The journey to Jerusalem, even though Nehemiah probably took the shortest route possible, would take at least two months. And no sooner did he arrive (perhaps even before he arrived) than he began to face opposition from the enemies of Israel. When Sanballat, the governor of Samaria, and his associate, Tobiah, heard that Nehemiah "had come to seek the welfare of the sons of Israel" (2:10), they were unhappy. Immediately they began to plan how to stop Nehemiah from achieving his goal. But Nehemiah's motivation remained undaunted. He knew God had brought him to this moment in Israel's history and he was about to tackle a project that others before him— for almost 150 years—had been unable to complete.

Nehemiah Surveys the City (Neh. 2:11-16)

Even though his two-month journey must have been terribly exhausting, Nehemiah wasted little time when he arrived in Jerusalem. Knowing how he worked, I believe he must have spent three days asking questions and discovering the present status of his people. Obviously, it would not take long to confirm in his own mind what he had heard six months earlier from his brother, Hanani, and several other men who had journeyed to Susa to give him the dismal report (see 1:2,3). Morale among his Jewish brethren *was* low. Discouragement permeated the ranks of Israel.

Nehemiah knew there was no way he could share with his people what he planned to accomplish without first doing some very careful research and planning. His strategy involved taking a few men into his confidence, men he could trust.

Then be began a careful survey of the walls in order to analyze the problem he faced (see 2:13). "And I arose in the night," Nehemiah later wrote, "I and a few men with me. I did not tell any one what my God was putting in my mind to do for Jerusalem. . . . And the officials did not know where I had gone or what I had done; nor had I as yet told the Jews, the priests, the nobles, the officials or the rest who did the work" (2:12,16). During the night hours Nehemiah gained perspective, and as we'll see in our next chapter, he put together an amazing plan to accomplish the task he had come to Jerusalem to perform.

Nehemiah Challenges the People (Neh. 2:17-20)

Once Nehemiah had completed his secret survey and was satisfied in his own mind that he had developed a workable plan, he knew the time had come to reveal to the children of Israel why he had actually come to Jerusalem. This he must have done with unusual wisdom and intense enthusiasm. First, he challenged them to join him in doing something about their deplorable circumstances. "Come," he said, "let us rebuild the wall of Jerusalem that we may no longer be a reproach" (2:17).

You can imagine the negative thoughts and feelings

that must have intensified in the hearts of the Jews when they first heard Nehemiah's initial challenge. Rebuild the walls? They must have thought Nehemiah was crazy or on some kind of ego trip! In their own minds they must have viewed Nehemiah's challenge as an impossible task. Didn't Nehemiah know what was going on? Hadn't he heard about their terrible situation? Didn't he understand that King Artaxerxes had issued the decree against them, stopping the work?

From a human perspective rebuilding the wall *was* an impossible task. Their negative reactions were predictable. But Nehemiah's perspective was more than human. Already he had experienced what God could do in a situation that seemed totally hopeless. And seemingly before his fellow Jews could even voice their negative feelings, he quickly went on to report how God had already helped him. "And I told them," he wrote, "how the hand of my God had been favorable to me, and also about the king's words which he had spoken to me" (2:18).

Somewhere in the process of Nehemiah's report, negative feelings turned positive. Despair turned to hope. Together and with enthusiasm they said, "Let us arise and build." And thus we read that "they put their hands to the good work" (2:18). With the help of God Nehemiah had rallied the people to attack the problem head-on.

Once again we see a beautiful illustration of God's involvement in human affairs. And the unique balance between the Lord's divine help and human responsibility is obvious. Earlier Nehemiah had reported that he had been successful because *the good hand of his God was on him* (see 2:8). And now in verse 18 we read, "So *they* put *their hands* to the good work." And this is the way it has always been when God's people are achieving true spiritual objectives. *God's hand* is at work through *human hands*.

Word spread rapidly regarding Israel's decision to

rebuild the walls. And as soon as the enemies of Israel heard the news they stepped up their efforts to hinder the process. They "mocked" them and "despised" them. They used every demoralizing technique they knew, including an old decree of King Artaxerxes. Even though Sanballat and Tobiah must have known that Nehemiah had been granted permission by the king to rebuild the walls, they tried to use outdated information to achieve their own selfish goals (see 2:19).

Nehemiah was ready for their insidious attack! Stepping forward, he faced their verbal abuse with bold words of his own. *"The God of heaven* will give us success," he responded; "therefore we His servants *will* arise and build, but you have no portion, right, or memorial in Jerusalem" (2:20).

Once again Nehemiah brought the task—both in the eyes of Israel and his enemies—into clear focus. *Their dependence was not primarily on their own human abilities, their human resources or their personal genius. Their hope was in the God of Abraham, Isaac and Jacob!*

How Balanced Are You?

The lessons we can learn from Nehemiah's initial days in Jerusalem, Nehemiah 2:9-20, continue the same basic theme illustrated in 2:1-8: *as Christians we must maintain a proper balance between divine and human factors in doing the will of God on earth.* Nehemiah had prepared himself thoroughly for that moment when Artaxerxes made inquiry about his dejected countenance. Well thought through answers were on the tip of his tongue. And even in the process of dialoguing with the king, Nehemiah quietly prayed for divine guidance in order to utilize his preparation wisely.

The same process is illustrated in Nehemiah's life once he arrived in Jerusalem. If he were to convince the children of Israel that they should "arise and build," he needed to thoroughly prepare a strategy ahead of time and then unveil the plan with discretion and wisdom. Furthermore, his greatest challenge was to convince them that the task was not in *their hands* alone. Rather they would only be able to rebuild the walls if *God's good hand* continued to be upon them. To get his point across, he shared with them his own experience with Artaxerxes. Convinced, they responded.

How can we flesh out this principle in our lives as twentieth-century Christians? As stated in the previous chapter, we must continually put forth conscious effort to maintain a proper balance between relying upon *God* and our own *human efforts*. This process in itself, of course, calls for "human effort." It doesn't happen automatically. God places a significant amount of responsibility on us for maintaining this balance. At this point the scale that so intricately balances *God's sovereignty* and *human responsibility* is weighted in our direction.

At our disposal we have His divine and supernatural resources—the Bible, the Holy Spirit and prayer. He has also provided us with many human and natural resources—other Christians, general knowledge, our own intelligence and experiential backgrounds. But whether or not to use these divine and human resources is ours to decide. God has not promised to automatically resolve our problems without intensive effort on our part. Even Bible study and prayer involve self-discipline and personal sacrifice. This has already been dramatically illustrated in Nehemiah's life, for he spent many weeks fasting and praying, preparing for that moment when he was asked that critical and crucial question by Artaxerxes which was to affect the course of history for the Jews in Jerusalem.

A New Testament example. Paul's concern for unity among Christians illustrates this divine *and* human process. There is no question that all Christians who put their faith in Christ are *one* in Christ. Writing to the Ephesians,

Paul made this point clear when he described the relationship between Jews and Gentiles once they become believers. Speaking specifically to the Gentile believers, he said: "Remember that you were at that time [before your conversion] separate from Christ, excluded from the commonwealth of Israel, and strangers to the covenants of promise, having no hope and without God in the world. But now in Christ Jesus you who formerly were far off have been brought near by the blood of Christ" (Eph. 2:12,13).

Paul then made his major point very clear: "For He Himself is our peace, who made both groups into one" (v. 14). Christ has broken down the dividing wall so that "He might make the two into *one new man* . . . and might reconcile them *both in one body*" (vv. 15,16).

It is very apparent from these statements that *in Christ* Christians are all one. This is automatic upon conversion. But the fact remains that this is a *positional* truth. This unity exists in God's heart and mind; it is a theological reality. But in this historical setting this doctrinal reality still needed to be fleshed out in the lives of these first-century Christians.

How was this to take place? Again Paul made his point clear as he moved into the practical section of his letter beginning in chapter 4. "I, therefore, the prisoner of the Lord, entreat you to walk in a manner worthy of the calling with which you have been called, . . . *being diligent to preserve the unity of the Spirit* in the bond of peace" (4:1,3).

The rest of Paul's letter is replete with instructions on how to maintain this unity. It would only happen if these Christians did everything they could to cause it to happen. In this sense, the responsibility for practical and visible unity in the church lay squarely on the shoulders of these believers.

A twentieth-century illustration. A tendency for Christians to go to extremes in the outworking of theological realities became very clear to me one day as I participated in a faculty discussion at Dallas Theological Seminary. At that time we were projecting a multi-million dollar campus development program. We had sent out some initial communication to friends of the seminary, explaining our intent. The response was meager. One faculty member who was well known for his strong views on God's sovereign control of the universe and who was usually rather verbal against any kind of promotional effort, spoke out rather forthrightly. "It appears God is telling us not to build since we're getting so little financial response from our friends." My response to his comment was just as outspoken. "It may also indicate," I said, "that *we* have failed to do *our part* in letting people know how important this project is to our future effectiveness."

The facts are that once we began to do a better job in the promotional and developmental areas of our school, people began to respond. Today, as of this writing, several phases of this initial proposal have been realized with the culmination of the total project in close range. God honored our *human* efforts *plus* our prayers and faith in Him.

A delicate balance. Please don't misunderstand. And don't criticize my professor friend. I too firmly believe in God's sovereignty. He *does* control the affairs of men. But I also know the Bible is filled with illustrations and instructions regarding human responsibility. And I also know from biblical examples and personal experience that *how* we respond to opportunities that lie before us and *what we do* as God's children does make a difference. While in Susa, Nehemiah could have prayed and not prepared when he received the report from Jerusalem. If he had, he would not have been ready to face Artaxerxes' interrogation. And when he arrived in Jerusalem, he could have prayed and trusted God and not surveyed the walls which enabled him to prepare his intricate plan. If he had only prayed, the people would have been frustrated. The project would have failed—unless God raised up another man who would both "pray *and* prepare," which He would have done because of His promises to Israel.

The same observation applies to us. That day in our faculty discussion, if we had listened to a professor friend who seemed to believe that if it were God's will He would make it possible for us to construct buildings without more diligent effort on our part, the project would never have gotten off the drawing board.

I must hasten to add, however, that if our efforts had not been bathed in prayer, if we had not trusted God and sought His will in the Word, the project might never have been possible either. And if we had succeeded in doing it without God's help, we would be merely building a monument to man rather than to God. And if we had not maintained that intricate balance, His ultimate blessings would not be upon us.

Life Response

It is true that these great realities are difficult to comprehend and reconcile in our finite minds. God's sovereignty and man's free will remain a great mystery—an antinomy. Both are true, but they cannot be defined and explained in a satisfactory manner to human beings. From a purely human perspective, they appear as irreconcilable concepts. And those who spend countless hours trying to explain these things thoroughly frequently go to extremes, ignoring one point of view or the other.

What about you? The following pairs of statements will help you evaluate your own approach to the matter and to detect whether or not you are violating the intricate balance God wants us to maintain. Each statement in the pair reflects an extreme point of view. Check to see if your personal views fall into one category or another.

1. ☐ When I read and study the Scriptures, I see primarily an emphasis on God's sovereign control of the universe.

    ☐ When I read and study the Scriptures, I see primarily an emphasis on human responsibility.

2. ☐ The concept of God's sovereignty is in my mind constantly.

    ☐ The concept of human responsibility as a Christian is constantly in my thoughts.

3. ☐ I tend to resent people who always talk about human responsibility.

    ☐ I tend to resent people who always talk about God's sovereignty.

4. ☐ I find it easy to withdraw from human involvement in the lives of people because of my view of God's sovereignty.

    ☐ I constantly have a sense of guilt because I do not have enough time in the day to do everything that needs to be done in ministering to the needs of people.

5. ☐ I am more concerned that Christians know about God's sovereign election for salvation than that they know they are responsible to carry out the Great Commission.

    ☐ I am more concerned that Christians be involved in carrying out the Great Commission than that they understand God's sovereign election in salvation.

6. ☐ I pray because God wants me to, though I really believe that what will happen will happen because of God's sovereign involvement in our lives.

    ☐ If prayer does not change things, I believe it is always because of a lack of faith on our part and an improper spiritual perspective.

7. ☐ I do not believe that God will hold us responsible for people who eventually go to hell because they have never heard about Christ.

    ☐ I believe that God will hold us responsible for the

souls of those who go to hell—that their blood will be required at our hands.

8. ☐ I believe that those who will be saved will be saved; that missionaries are not necessary.

☐ I believe that men will be lost eternally because Christians have not been missionaries.

NOTE: If you have checked most of the first items in each set of statements, you are probably going to an extreme on what the Bible teaches about God's "sovereignty." If you checked most of the second items in each set of statements, you are probably going to an extreme on "human responsibility."

A Follow-up Project

If you were to reword these statements to represent a balanced view in Scripture, how would you state each concept?

4

Nehemiah's
Comprehensive Plan

Nehemiah 3:1-32

Chapter 3 in the book of Nehemiah is one that is easy to pass over. Like a number of Old Testament accounts, it is filled with names that are difficult to pronounce, information that seems unusually redundant, and chronology that initially appears rather meaningless.

From my own personal study of the Bible, I've discovered that these observations and feelings—and I've had them all—only represent my human limitations. Inherent in chapter 3 are the results of Nehemiah's nightly survey and very careful planning. In the midst of telling the story of *how* the walls were actually rebuilt, Nehemiah jumps ahead in the process and, in looking back, succinctly tells us how it was actually accomplished.

A Geographical Perspective

To this point in this study we've discussed the walls of Jerusalem without visual perspective. To understand more fully the chapter before us it's imperative that we *see* as well as *hear*. Notice the map in figure 3. Because of limited archeological evidence, it merely *represents* the actual geographical setting, but it represents well the main outline which Nehemiah used to write chapter 3. As you study the map, begin at 12:00 and move counterclockwise, following the direction of the arrows. As you move around the walls, you will notice that most of the specific places identified on the way are actually mentioned in chronological order in chapter 3, beginning with the Sheep Gate in verse 1 and ending with the Muster Gate in verse 31.

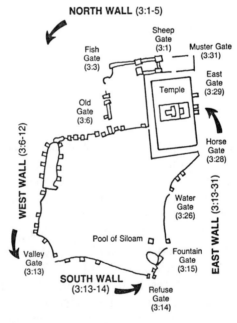

Figure 3
Jerusalem in the time of Nehemiah

Lessons in Leadership

There are at least three dynamic lessons in leadership that emerge from this chapter. Cyril Barber identifies them as: *Coordination, Cooperation,* and *Commendation.*[1] Using these principles as guidelines, let me highlight several observations.

The Principle of Coordination

A task so enormous as rebuilding the walls of Jerusalem, especially under such adverse conditions, called for unusual organizational effort by Nehemiah. Together with the small band of men he took into his confidence, he must have worked night and day putting together his plan.

Every person must be in his place. This unusual coordination stands out in chapter 3 with such phrases as "next to him," or "next to them," and "after him" or "after them." If you will take a pencil and underscore in your Bible these phrases you'll find they are recorded 28 times in this chapter, in 21 of the 32 verses (for example, see the following passage).

> 1 Then Eliashib the high priest arose with his brothers the priests and built the Sheep Gate: they consecrated it and hung its doors. They consecrated the wall to the Tower of the Hundred and the Tower of Hananel.
>
> 2 And *next to him* the men of Jericho built, and *next to them* Zaccur the son of Imri built.
>
> 3 Now the sons of Hassenaah built the Fish Gate; they laid its beams and hung its doors with its bolts and bars.
>
> 4 And *next to them* Meremoth the son of Uriah, the son of Hakkoz made repairs. And *next to him* Meshullam the son of Berechiah the son of Meshezabel made repairs. And *next to him* Zadok the son of Baana also made repairs.

> 5 Moreover, *next to him* the Tekoites made repairs, but their nobles did not support the work of their masters.

Putting everyone in his place reflects phenomenal coordination of effort. And of course it didn't just happen. And it *never* happens that way. What may appear to be a smooth-running operation always involves careful planning behind the scenes. This was not some spontaneous movement of God's Spirit that suddenly put every man and woman in a particular place around the wall, doing certain things. It involved hours and hours of careful research, thought and planning. And once people were in their places they needed *proper supervision* to know how to do the job, as well as *adequate resources*. All of this had to be thought through ahead of time. Coordination involves preliminary effort, followed by comprehensive communication. And when all of this is guided and directed by God Himself, as it was in this instance, you have the unique balance we've already observed so thoroughly between "God's hand" and "men's hands" working together.

Assignment was made by residence. Another clue to the principle of coordination which Nehemiah applied is revealed in the following statements:

> 21 . . . from the doorway of Eliashib's house even as far as *the end of his house* . . . .
>
> 23 After them Benjamin and Hasshub carried out repairs *in front of their house*. After them Azariah the son of Maaseiah, son of Ananiah carried out repairs *beside his house*.
>
> 24 After him Binnui the son of Henadad repaired another section, *from the house of Azariah* . . . .
>
> 28 Above the Horse Gate the priests carried

out repairs, each *in front of his house*.

29 After them Zadok the son of Immer carried out repairs *in front of his house* . . . .

30 After him Meshullam the son of Berechiah carried out repairs *in front of his own quarters*.

The implications of this plan are obvious: (1) people who were assigned to sections of the wall near their homes would be more personally involved and consequently more highly motivated; (2) they would not have to travel to another part of the city to do the job, wasting valuable time; and (3) in case of attack they would not be tempted to leave their posts, but would stay and protect their families. Furthermore, the whole task would be a family effort, utilizing all available talent. As Barber observes, "By arranging for each man to work close to his own home, Nehemiah made it easy for them to get to work, to be sustained while on the job, and to safeguard those who were nearest and dearest to them. This relieved each worker of any unnecessary anxiety. It also insured that each person would put his best effort into what he was doing."[2]

The commuters also had a part. The opposite side of the city tells the "other side" of the story and compliments the unique strategy just outlined. The men whose homes were outside of Jerusalem—in Jericho, Tekoa, Gibeon, and Mizpah—were assigned to sections of the wall where there were few homes (see 3:2,5,7). They were obviously commuters, and were asked to complete tasks that could not be as conveniently handled by the permanent residents in Jerusalem. This again was ingenious planning.

Nehemiah also assigned work location by vocation. Some Bible interpreters have suggested that Nehemiah assigned specific people to designated areas that related to their special vocations. Though this is a more speculative observation, it was definitely true of the priests. "Eliashib the high priest" and "his brothers" were assigned to rebuild the "Sheep Gate" (3:1), which would be of particular interest to them, since it was through this gate that animals were brought to the temple for sacrifice.

There are no doubt other clues in this chapter which point to Nehemiah's careful and cautious planning which resulted in this almost incredible coordinated effort. But we've looked at enough to gain significant insight into this man's unusual administrative skills. Let's look next at the second reason why the children of Israel were able to rebuild the walls against impossible odds.

The Principle of Cooperation

We've already observed in chapter 2 that the children of Israel responded in *corporate* fashion to Nehemiah's challenge. "Let *us* arise and build" (v. 18), they said. With few exceptions, they *all* responded to Nehemiah's request. And chapter 3 verifies that this was not an initial response which was only verbal in nature and motivated by the emotions of the moment. The children of Israel fleshed out their words with actions. They were not only hearers but doers; and most important, *everyone* was involved.

It is clear that Nehemiah needed to choose certain experienced and qualified men to supervise the rebuilding of certain sections of the wall. In some instances this appears, as we've already seen, to be the heads of households. But it also seems that there were sections of the wall that were also supervised by "officials" who were already experienced men in their own right. This is obvious from the following references:

> 9 . . .Rephaiah . . ., the official of half the district of Jerusalem, made repairs.
> 12 . . .Shallum . . ., the official of half the

district of Jerusalem, made repairs. . .

14 . . .Malchijah . . ., the official of the district of Beth-haccherem, repaired the Refuse Gate. . .

15 Shallum . . ., the official of the district of Mizpah, repaired the Fountain Gate. . .

16 . . .Nehemiah . . ., official of half the district of Beth-zur, made repairs. . .

17 . . .Hashabiah, the official of half the district of Keilah, carried out repairs for his district.

18 . . .Bavvai . . ., official of the other half of the district of Keilah.

19 . . .Ezer . . ., the official of Mizpah repaired another section.

If you've ever worked with men and women in middle or top management positions you'll quickly realize that these people are sometimes less cooperative with one another than people generally. There are various reasons for this, but one involves the fact that they are recognized in their own right as people with management responsibility. They are used to making decisions and issuing orders.

In a sense the "officials" mentioned in this chapter represent middle or top management people. Yet, Nehemiah succeeded in getting all of these men to cooperate wholeheartedly in supervising the rebuilding of certain gates and sections of the wall. This represents a significant administrative accomplishment.

Nehemiah's record in chapter 3 also points out that men and women of all ages and from all walks of life participated. There were "priests" (3:1); "goldsmiths" (3:8); "perfumers" (3:8); "temple servants" (3:26); and "merchants" (3:32). In a special note, Nehemiah must have felt it was important to mention that Shallum, an official of Jerusalem, worked side by side with "his *daugh-*

ters" (3:12). And indeed this is significant! This indicates that whole families worked together to rebuild certain sections of the wall.

There were few exceptions. Generally speaking, everyone cooperated. But there *were* exceptions. There always are in any project involving people. Some have good reasons, others have poor reasons. And it appears Nehemiah faced this very normal problem. In verse 5 we read that, "The Tekoites made repairs, *but* their nobles did not support the work of of their masters". Why, we do not know. As an elite group of individuals, they maybe felt they were above getting their hands dirty. Perhaps they didn't feel it was their responsibility since they lived outside Jerusalem. They may not have wanted to make the sacrifice. Perhaps they were afraid to identify with the children of Israel and face the harassment from their enemies. They may have just been selfish. But whatever their motives, they represent those few who, without good reasons, do not become involved.

But this was the exception not the rule. And Nehemiah did not allow their negative response to interfere with his own motivation nor the desire of others to complete the task. The end result verifies that fact. The job was eventually completed because almost everyone cooperated and did what he could.

The Principle of Commendation

There is another important leadership quality that characterized Nehemiah. He was an *encourager*. In chapter 3 it is more implied than stated. This of course is natural, for Nehemiah who recorded this account would not state this about himself.

The most obvious evidence that he was an encourager is that he appears as a people person. In this chapter alone he mentioned *75* people by name and in many instances recognized their accomplishments. He also mentioned at least 15 *groups* of people—such as the priests, Levites, the goldsmiths, the perfumers, and the temple servants—and a number of groups from other towns and cities. This indicates that Nehemiah knew these people by name. He knew not only where they worked, but also what they had accomplished (and eventually recognized it in writing).

One very significant statement—very easy to miss—is hidden away in this mass of specific data in chapter 3. It involves one name and one word! In verse 20 Nehemiah recorded that "Baruch the son of Zabbai *zealously* repaired another section" (3:20). Here was a man who stood out above the others. How? Maybe he worked overtime, for nothing. Maybe he worked faster and harder. Maybe he bypassed some of his coffee breaks. Maybe he at times worked around the clock! We really don't know for sure, but we do know he was special, and Nehemiah recognized it, even in eternal writ.

I remember hearing Tom Landry, longtime coach of the Dallas Cowboys, speak several years ago after they won their first Super Bowl. He commended the whole team in various ways, but especially one man—Roger Staubach—the successful Cowboy quarterback. "Roger always puts forth that extra effort," he said. "When the men end practice with so many required laps around the field, Roger always makes at least one more than everyone else. He's just that kind of hardworking person," commented Landry. And, of course, it paid off for Roger Staubach and the whole team.

But the point I'm making is that Tom Landry let the world know about that extra effort. And that is what Nehemiah did with Baruch. And don't you suppose Zabbai, his father, who was also named, was very excited to be identified with his son's extra effort! It's obvious that Nehemiah practiced the principle of commendation! Yes, he mentioned a select few for special recognition, but he also did all he could to recognize everyone he possibly could, no matter what their accomplishment.

Applying These Principles Today

Nehemiah's example in planning raises some very personal and thought-provoking questions.

1. To what extent do you "plan your work" and "work your plan"—and at the same time recognize God as your divine resource person? Effective planning is absolutely essential, no matter what our vocation in life. There is no task that can be done well without careful forethought. Whether husband, wife—or parent—a successful home is a result of good management. In fact, the ability to manage the home is stated clearly as a requirement for those who seek leadership roles in the church (1 Tim. 3:4,5). And, of course, this implies that a church must also be carefully managed. Elders and pastors must plan God's work diligently.

It is also true that no vocation in the business world exempts employees from being good planners. Whether part of the management team or a member of the support staff, planning is at the heart of every task.

The plan, however, may be only some well organized ideas on paper. It is one thing to write out goals; it is another to achieve them. It is one thing to have a job description; it is yet another to translate these responsibilities and ideas into action. We must both "plan our work" and "work our plan."

But there is a third factor for every Christian. Most anyone can plan; and if motivated, most anyone can "work that plan." But a Christian, to be truly successful, must balance that effort with prayer and faith in God. Nehemiah, of course, exemplified this process.

2. To what extent are you involved in your church—doing your part—utilizing your talent, your abilities, your personal resources? As we have seen, the task in Jerusalem was completed because nearly everyone participated. Everyone contributed what he could. This will be demonstrated even more clearly in the chapters to come.

As we move into the New Testament, God emphasizes the importance of total participation even more so than in the Old Testament. The apostle Paul especially outlined God's plan. He used an analogy to get his point across, the analogy of the human body. In order for the Body of Christ—the church—to grow and mature and to function properly so that it might build itself up in love, "every joint" must supply; "each individual part" must do its work (Eph. 4:16).

How beautifully this was illustrated in Jerusalem as *together* the children of Israel rebuilt the walls. But how much more important it is when this principle is applied to the church. We are a "spiritual house" (1 Pet. 2:5). We are "God's household, having been built upon the foundation of the apostles and the prophets, Christ Jesus Himself being the cornerstone, in whom the whole building, being fitted together is growing into a holy temple in the Lord" (Eph. 2:19-21). For this process to take place, every Christian must participate. Everyone is needed. "We, who are many, are one body in Christ, and individually *members one of another*" (Rom. 12:5).

3. To what extent are you an encourager—a real people person? Generally speaking, Christians do not tend to encourage one another as they should. And yet few biblical concepts are emphasized and repeated more often than this one. And no concept is more important than helping others to consistently do the will of God.

Barnabas stands out in the New Testament as a primary example of a Christian who encouraged others. In fact, he was named Barnabas by the apostles because it means "Son of Encouragement" (Acts 4:36). Obviously, his name reflected what he actually was.

There are various reasons why Christians do not encourage one another as they should. For one thing, we don't realize how important it is. If we did, we would do more of it.

Another reason is that some of us have a false view of what it will do to others. We are afraid it will create pride, when in actuality encouragement helps people to ultimately overcome tendencies towards pride.

It is unfortunate that many people who do not encourage others are so much in need of it themselves they resort to reaction formation. They sometimes become critical and discouraging. They are so occupied with themselves and their own weaknesses and needs that they try to tear others down. This is indeed unfortunate.

Christians, of all people, should encourage others. Not to do so is to directly disobey specific commands of Scripture. "Therefore *encourage one another,* and build up one another" wrote Paul to the Thessalonians (1 Thess. 5:11). And the author of the Hebrews letter (who some believe was Barnabas) is even more specific: "Let us consider how to stimulate one another to love and good deeds, not forsaking our own assembling together, as is the habit of some but *encouraging one another;* and all the more, as you see the day drawing near" (Heb. 10:24,25).

When I became the director of the evening school at Moody Bible Institute in Chicago, where I served on the faculty for 13 years, I was faced with a great challenge. For a number of years, no one had given specific direction to this very significant work. Because it was a part of the overall structure, it rumbled on for some time and was relatively successful without too much guidance. When I took over its leadership, we were ministering to nearly 700 to 800 students from all over the Chicago area.

The major problem I faced, however, was one of morale among the teachers. Most of these people were members of the day school faculty and viewed this evening school assignment as a rather burdensome responsibility. This is understandable: these were evening classes, and most of the teachers were physically drained from teaching during the daylight hours. Furthermore, the students who made up these classes in evening school were working people. By evening they were also rather tired.

Fairly early in the history of my directorship, I began visiting various churches in the greater Chicago area. Invariably I would meet evening school students. I remember on one occasion meeting a student who voluntarily mentioned to me how much one of the professors in the evening school had meant to her. Though the student was always weary when she arrived at school after a long day working in the office, and even though she at times struggled to stay awake during class, she shared that she wouldn't miss the experience. "It's changing my life," she said.

I wrote down the student's name and the name of the professor. The next day (Monday) when I arrived in my own office, I called him by phone and relayed to him what the student had shared. "Well, thanks," he said—quite pleasantly surprised.

"Well, thank you, Chuck," I replied. "I appreciate you, too."

I soon discovered that honest feedback like this began to change these teachers' whole outlook on their evening school ministry. I also found out that this kind of encouragement was the first that some had ever received from their superiors, though they had been teaching for years.

How tragic! Sincere and honest encouragement is so easy, so inexpensive—so powerful and motivating. Listen to these verses from Proverbs.
• "Anxiety in the heart of a man weighs it down, but a *good word* makes it glad" (Prov. 12:25).

• *"Pleasant words* are a honeycomb, sweet to the soul and healing to the bones" (Prov. 16:24).
• "Like apples of gold in settings of silver is a *word spoken* in right circumstances" (Prov. 25:11).

Life Response

Evaluate your own life in the light of Nehemiah's example and these New Testament correlations and applications. The following checklist will help you.

I have a specific procedure for planning my work such as:

☐ Writing out goals and standards for the month, the week and the day
☐ Making a priority list at the beginning of each day
☐ Spending specific time doing nothing but planning

I evaluate my effectiveness in "working my plan," such as:

☐ Measuring my activities and accomplishments against my goals and standards
☐ Having others help evaluate my performance
☐ Taking special classes and refresher courses to improve my effectiveness

I not only use my human resources but also draw on God's divine resources, such as:

☐ Asking God for wisdom and guidance as I plan
☐ Asking God for both wisdom and strength as I work out my plans
☐ Evaluating my plans and accomplishments by means of biblical injunctions and principles

I'm an active participant in the Body of Christ by:

☐ Realizing I am important to other members of the Body of Christ (Rom. 12:5)
☐ Being devoted to others in brotherly love (Rom. 12:10)
☐ Honoring others above myself (Rom. 12:10)
☐ Working to produce unity in the Body (Rom. 15:5)
☐ Accepting others as Christ accepted me (Rom. 15:7)

☐ Admonishing others in love (Rom. 15:14)
☐ Greeting others sincerely (Rom. 16:16)
☐ Serving others (Gal. 5:13)
☐ Carrying others' burdens (Gal. 6:2)
☐ Being tolerant toward others (Eph. 4:2)
☐ Submitting to others (Eph. 5:21)

I am an "encourager" of others. This is obvious because:

☐ I tell people thank you when they minister to me personally.
☐ I give positive feedback to people when I hear others express appreciation.
☐ I tell people I'm praying for them.
☐ I ask people what prayer needs they have.
☐ I write notes of appreciation.
☐ I look for discouraged people and give them a word of encouragement.
☐ I make an effort to reach out to lonely people.
☐ I respond to others' needs with love and gentleness.

Notes

1. Cyril Barber, *Nehemiah and the Dynamics of Effective Leadership* (Neptune, NJ: Loizeaux Brothers, 1976), pp. 49-54.
2. Ibid., p. 49.

5

Nehemiah
Faces Discouragement

Nehemiah 4:1-6

Simply reading chapter 3 of Nehemiah might give the impression that once Nehemiah had carefully and wisely assigned everyone to a particular section of the wall, from that point forward everything progressed smoothly, without difficulty. Not so! God's work *never* goes forward without opposition. Satan sees to that. And what Nehemiah records next in his story clearly describes this opposition. The primary focus of that opposition centers on Sanballat, the governor of Samaria. We've already met him twice before in Nehemiah's narrative.

As we follow the flow of this story, we've seen that Nehemiah 3 is a parenthetical summary of the methods Nehemiah used to begin the job of rebuilding the walls and how the task was eventually accomplished. This is his organizational and administrative point of view. Now in

Nehemiah 4 we pick up where the story ended in chapter 2, with Sanballat's, Tobiah's and Geshem's opposition (2:19, 20; 4:1-3). We now discover more specifically what happened.

Sanballat's Psychological Warfare (Neh. 4:1-3)

When Sanballat heard via the "oppositional grapevine" that Nehemiah was on his way "to seek the welfare of the sons of Israel," he was very displeased (see 2:10). But once Nehemiah actually arrived in Jerusalem and rallied the Jews to begin rebuilding the walls, Sanballat's displeasure intensified (see 2:19).

Initially it appears his emotional discomfort was more related to what we might classify as a minor irritation that goes along naturally with being a political leader. He probably found it difficult to take very seriously Nehemiah's presence in Jerusalem. After all, what could one man do, even *with* the king's approval? History was on Sanballat's side. For many years the Jews had failed to rebuild Jerusalem.

His Limited Perspective

There was one very important factor in Sanballat's historical perspective that was missing. He did not understand God's personal interest in the children of Israel— that is, that their failure and years in captivity related to their sin against the Lord but that their restoration related to their repentance and renewed obedience to his commands. This indeed was why Nehemiah had gained favor with King Artaxerxes. He and others in Israel who had not followed false gods confessed Israel's sins and prayed for restoration to their land (see 1:8-11).

With this limited perspective, Sanballat's reactions are predictable. Once Nehemiah arrived in Jerusalem and succeeded in building his people's morale and organizing them for the task, what was at first a minor irritation to

Sanballat turned into a very significant threat. His displeasure turned to anger. Nehemiah records: "Now it came about that when Sanballat heard that we were rebuilding the wall, he became *furious* and *very angry*" (4:1).

Threat usually creates one of two basic reactions—fear and retreat, or anger and aggression—and in most instances there is a mixture of both. There is no question as to which was Sanballat's *primary* response. He became intensely angry· and aggressive. But it was also anger mixed with fear, for he did not initially attack the children of Israel with military force. His warfare was psychological. His reactions in themselves give us some interesting clues into Sanballat's personality weaknesses as well as the weaknesses of those who supported him.

His Defense Mechanisms

The first clue is reflected in his behavior before his own friends. "He spoke in the presence of his brothers and the wealthy men of Samaria and said, 'What are these feeble Jews doing? Are they going to restore it for themselves? Can they offer sacrifices? Can they finish in a day? Can they revive the stones from the dusty rubble even the burned ones?' " (4:2).

This does not sound like a secure man. Every question reflects the fact that he was trying to convince *himself* that there was no danger. On the surface he sounded tough and in charge. Underneath, he was worried and intensely frightened.

Psychologists call this kind of behavior *reaction formation*. Because of deep anxiety, we reflect the opposite of what we really feel. Had Sanballat been honest with himself he would have responded differently to what was happening in Jerusalem, even in his anger. His report before his friends may have gone something like this:

Nehemiah is a man to be reckoned with. He's no fool. Under his leadership these Jews are

really serious about rebuilding the walls.
They're not as feeble as we think. They're
actually planning to restore Jerusalem so they
can live comfortably in the city and once again
offer sacrifices to their God. And they're not
wasting any time. They plan to complete the
task as soon as possible, actually rebuilding it
from dusty rubble. And with access to the
king's forest, we've got a serious problem. If
they accomplish this task, they'll threaten our
whole economy.

Unfortunately for Sanballat, his closest associate—
Tobiah the Ammonite—didn't help him much. He only
reinforced Sanballat's superficial approach to the problem. Standing next to him, Tobiah responded, Right on,
Sanballat! "Even what they are building—if a fox should
jump on it, he would break their stone wall down!" (4:3).

This is another defense mechanism—*identification*. In
order to bolster his own position with Sanballat, Tobiah
refused to be honest with himself *and* Sanballat and
allowed him to go on in his self-deception. This, of
course, is one reason why a mature leader does not build
around himself yes-men who are merely seeking a position
of prominence and who will compromise the truth in order
to be accepted and promoted. Had Tobiah been mature and
a *true* friend, he would have responded to Sanballat's
emotional outbursts something like this:

Sanballat, I know how you feel. Your anger is
understandable. I am amazed at what is happening, and fearful. But these Jews are serious.
And we've got to take them seriously. They
may appear feeble but that's because they've
had no leader. They've been demoralized, but
Nehemiah has changed all that. They *do* plan to
restore Jerusalem and once again offer sacrifices. Maybe we'd better think twice before

we fight against Israel—and their God. Don't you remember their history? They accomplished some unbelievable feats when they first settled this land. As I remember they achieved these victories in the name of the same God Nehemiah claims caused him to have compassion for King Artaxerxes.

Had Sanballat and Tobiah responded maturely to the miracle that was taking shape in Jerusalem before their very eyes, they might have been converted to the one true God. But because of their hard hearts and self-deception, they—and many others—brought themselves under the curse, which is reflected in Nehemiah's response to their psychological reactions.

Nehemiah's Spiritual Response (Neh. 4:4-6)

He prayed according to the will of God (see 4:4,5). Prayer was a distinct and consistent part of Nehemiah's approach to problem-solving. We've already observed that. When he first received the dismal report regarding the state of the Jews in Jerusalem, he immediately went to prayer (see 1:4). And now, when faced with Sanballat's demoralizing attack, he again goes to prayer. And as we'll see, he continued utilizing this divine resource throughout the total process of rebuilding the walls.

From a Christian point of view the content of Nehemiah's prayer is initially difficult to understand. Like some of David's imprecatory prayers in which he evoked evil on his enemies, Nehemiah's prayer in this instance is severe and condemning. He prayed: "Hear, O our God, how we are despised! Return their reproach on their own heads and give them up for plunder in a land of captivity. Do not forgive their iniquity and let not their sin be blotted out before Thee, for they have demoralized the builders" (4:4,5).

How do we interpret this kind of praying, especially in

view of what we are told by Jesus Christ and other writers of the New Testament? First, we must understand the content of this prayer. You see, God had already pronounced judgment on the enemies of Israel. That's why Nehemiah could confront Sanballat, a Samaritan, and others so confidently earlier in the story, telling them that they had "no portion, right, or memorial in Jerusalem" (2:20). The Lord had made it clear that Jerusalem belonged to His people—people who truly worshiped Him in spirit and in truth. And the same opportunity would have been given to Sanballat and others if they had responded to the truth. Many years later Jesus demonstrated this clearly when talking with *another Samaritan,* the woman at the well (see John 4:1-42). But Sanballat and his friends did not respond to God's grace. Consequently, God's judgment fell on them. Nehemiah then is simply praying according to God's will—that which God had already said would happen to the enemies of Israel (Josh. 1:5).

He continued with the work (see 4:6). Some people pray and wait for things to happen. Not Nehemiah! Like all of his effort thus far, he blended the divine perspective with the human. He put feet to his prayers. He faced Sanballat's psychological warfare with *both* prayer and hard work. Once he committed the problem to the Lord, he trusted God to help them to achieve their goal. And while praying and trusting, they "built the wall" and we read that "the whole wall was joined together to half its height" (4:6). At this juncture in the story, the job was half done.

But there is yet one more statement in this verse that deserves special attention. Israel continued to make progress in the midst of Sanballat's demoralizing efforts because "the people had a mind [literally a *heart*] to work" (4:6). They did not allow discouragement to break their internal fortitude and destroy their morale.

It is safe to conclude that Nehemiah's own enthusiasm and confidence in God were primary factors in helping these people keep their spirits high. Humanly speaking, they could not have continued without Nehemiah's continual encouragement.

However, by this time I believe the process became mutual and reciprocal. No doubt Israel's positive response to Nehemiah's leadership enabled him in turn to keep his own spirits high. Nothing succeeds like success. And once these people began to see the fruit of their efforts, they were able to encourage one another—and Nehemiah—to keep on going, in spite of Sanballat's demoralizing attitudes.

Handling Discouragement in the Twentieth-Century World

One of Satan's most common methods of hindering God's work is discouragement. When morale is low, God's work is seriously affected. And in the lives of individual Christians, discouragement becomes a serious hindrance to effective Christian ministry and service. For years this had happened in Jerusalem. The people of God were depressed, discouraged and demoralized. But with proper spiritual perspective and consequent action, they were able to rise above their negative circumstances and successfully do the will of God.

Nehemiah's spiritual formula will also work for twentieth-century Christians, particularly when it is applied in the full light of New Testament theology.

1. We must pray about uncomfortable situations. God is interested in every detail of our lives, especially our moments of discouragement and disappointment. Thus, Paul wrote, "Be anxious for nothing, but in *everything* by prayer and supplication with thanksgiving let your requests be made known to God" (Phil. 4:6).

I've seen the prayer process work frequently in my own life. In the ministry, I, like many others, often face times of discouragement and disappointment. I have discovered that if I pray specifically for encouragement, God invariably answers that prayer. Interestingly, He usually answers by sending another Christian my way to encourage me. What often amazes me is that the nature of the encouragement—the thing which is said or communicated—often relates specifically to the very thing creating the discouragement. My major shortcoming is that I don't utilize this divine resource enough. But when I do, God answers prayer. And this, of course, should not surprise me. It is in harmony with the promise that accompanies Paul's injunction to pray about anxious situations. And "the peace of God," he said, "which surpasses all comprehension, shall guard your hearts and your minds in Christ Jesus" (Phil. 4:7). As a Christian, are *you* utilizing this divine resource as you should? Remember, it's your privilege!

2. We must pray in the will of God. To understand how and what to pray as a twentieth-century Christian, we must have a total biblical perspective. It is only then that we can understand and comprehend praying in the will of God.

For example, the New Testament in no instance teaches us to pray down God's judgment on our enemies as Nehemiah or David did. In fact, it teaches the opposite. Is this contradictory? No. It simply involves understanding the will of God and praying in accordance with His will as God has revealed that will. David and Nehemiah were praying in God's will as He had revealed it to them directly relative to the children of Israel and their enemies at that time. And from God's full revelation as reflected in the New Testament, we can understand clearly the will of God in these matters, particularly in relationship to our enemies.

Jesus Christ made this very clear. "You have heard,"

He taught, "that it was said, 'You shall love your neighbor, and hate your enemy.' But I say to you, love your enemies, and pray for those who persecute you" (Matt. 5:43,44). And, of course, He illustrated this dramatically in His own life when He prayed for those who were mocking Him and at the same time nailing Him to the cross—"Father forgive them;" he prayed, "for they do not know what they are doing" (Luke 23:34).

Regarding a Christian's attitude towards his enemies, Paul also made the will of God clear in his letter to the Roman Christians. He wrote: "If possible, so far as it depends on you, be at peace with all men. Never take your own revenge, beloved, but leave room for the wrath of God, for it is written, 'Vengeance is Mine, I will repay, says the Lord. But if your enemy is hungry, feed him, and if he is thirsty, give him a drink; for in so doing you will heap burning coals upon his head.' Do not be overcome by evil, but overcome evil with good" (Rom. 12:18-21).

3. We must pray and work. Prayer alone is seldom God's plan for Christians when we face difficulties. Nehemiah graphically illustrates this for us in his own life. And it is illustrated by all of God's servants in the Bible. The Lord grants us the privilege to pray about *everything* but He also expects us to do *everything* we can to resolve our problems.

When it comes to discouragement, there are many things we can do immediately, even while we're in the process of praying. Following are several practical suggestions.

First, check your energy level both physically and emotionally. Nothing causes discouragement and lowers our ability to cope with problems more than exhaustion. Perhaps the first thing we need to do is to get some rest and relaxation.

We have a beautiful illustration of this principle in the

life of Elijah. After tremendous feats of faith against the prophets of Baal, he became so discouraged and depressed he wanted to die (see 1 Kings 19:4). The solution to Elijah's problem was quite simple and pragmatic. God allowed him to rest. We read that he lay down and slept. When he awakened, the Lord had prepared a meal for him. And once he had eaten, he slept again. When he awakened the second time, he had another meal. And after that we read that Elijah "went in the strength of that food forty days and forty nights" (1 Kings 19:8).

Second, make sure you are getting proper physical exercise. Unfortunately our twentieth-century culture is not designed to encourage people to get proper exercise. We drive to the store, drive around the block, drive to school, drive to church—which is a rather recent phenomenon in the history of the world.

On the other hand our culture is also designed so that most of us live under intense pressure—on the job, driving on expressways, keeping up with the Joneses, etc. *Little exercise* combined with *intense pressure* creates a lethal combination which can affect our physical and emotional energy levels. It is imperative that Christians develop some form of exercise to release emotional tension and stress. If we do not, we are much more vulnerable to stressful situations and we are less able to cope with factors that cause discouragement.

Third, spend some time with someone who is not discouraged. Nothing helps me out of the doldrums faster than to spend time with someone who is happy, excited and positive about life. On the other hand, it is devastating to spend time with a negative person when you're feeling negative yourself. In this case, two negatives *never* make a positive.

Fourth, do something for someone else. When you are discouraged, rather than sitting around feeling sorry for yourself, do something special for someone else. It is amazing how this in turn encourages you.

Fifth, accomplish a task. I sometimes get discouraged because of the volume of work I face. But I've also discovered I can often overcome that discouragement by attacking the work one task at a time. Sometimes, it only means completing a little task, and suddenly, I've gained some momentum emotionally, enabling me to attack larger problems and resolve them. And with each task completed, I feel more and more encouraged.

Sixth, attempt to learn important personal lessons from difficult situations. Remember that it is God's will that "all things . . . work together for good to those who love God, to those who are called according to His purpose" (Rom. 8:28). But this is not an automatic process. To experience the reality of this verse and this promise, we must look for the "good" in every situation, no matter how difficult it is.

I'm reminded of Dr. Viktor Frankl who, as an educated Jew, faced the ravages of a Nazi concentration camp. Like others around him, he was horribly depressed and discouraged and in a desperate state physically because of malnutrition. He actually felt as if he would die at any moment.

As a practicing psychiatrist before being taken captive by the Nazis, he had developed an approach to counseling called *logotherapy*. More specifically, he tried to help his patients see *meaning* in suffering.

He tells the story of how he utilized this approach on himself. The *only* meaning he could see in what was happening was that some day he would live to tell others that his therapy worked. He pictured in his mind a future day when he would be lecturing to a group of people on the subject of logotherapy, telling them how he survived those horrible experiences. By seeing this *meaning* in his experience, he was able to gain sufficient strength physically and emotionally to live to tell that story to thousands of people.

In fact, my wife and I heard him personally share the experience one evening in a special lectureship at the University of Dallas.

If this process worked for a man who does not claim to be a Christian, how much more should it work for a believer! What meaning can you see in your moment of discouragement? Is God preparing you to help someone else? Is He preparing you for greater responsibility? Will this make you a better parent, pastor or friend? By seeing meaning in difficult situations, you can become a more mature Christian and often rise above the negative emotions you are feeling.

Life Response

To what extent are you applying God's formula for overcoming discouragement? Check yourself.

☐ Do you pray specifically for encouragement?

☐ Do you pray for those who may be causing you to be discouraged?

☐ Do you take specific action steps to "put feet to your prayers"?

(Utilize the practical suggestions just given to discover what you have actually done to overcome discouragement.)

Write out one goal for your life right now that relates to the area of overcoming discouragement. (Perhaps your goal would be to help someone else who you know is discouraged.)

6

Nehemiah
Faces a Conspiracy

Nehemiah 4:7-15

Sanballat's initial attack on Nehemiah and the children of Israel was psychological. He succeeded in rallying to his cause Tobiah the Ammonite and Geshem the Arab and together they "mocked" and "despised" the Jews (2:19; 4:1). But their efforts at demoralization failed. The children of Israel rose above their attempts at discouragement. Because they had "a mind to work" (4:6) they were able to complete half the task in a surprisingly short period of time. Though we do not know exactly how much time it took to get to this point in the process, we do know that the whole task was completed in 52 days (see 6:15). If they had reached this half-way point approximately half way through this time period, they would have been at the job only about a month.

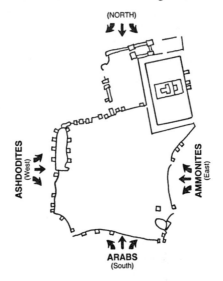

Figure 4
The Conspiracy Against Jerusalem

The Conspiracy Described (Neh. 4:7,8)

This rapid progress naturally increased the threat level for the enemies of Israel. When they received reports "that the repair of the walls of Jerusalem went on, and that the breaches began to be closed" (4:7) they knew they needed to take more overt and corporate action. Consequently, they "conspired together" (4:8) to attack Jerusalem from all sides—Sanballat and the Samaritans from the north, Tobiah and the Ammonites from the east, Geshem and the Arabs from the south and the Ashdodites from the west. Jerusalem was literally surrounded (see fig. 4).

A Corporate Response (Neh. 4:9)

The corporate strategy by Israel's enemies was met by a corporate response. This is very clear from Nehemiah's report of what happened. He wrote: "But *we* prayed to our God" (4:9). To this point it had been Nehemiah who had beseeched God for Israel's welfare. But now the *people* prayed.

How exciting and rewarding this must have been for Nehemiah! There is no evidence he had exhorted these people to pray. Evidently he had simply modeled the process and had demonstrated its effectiveness. And it appears when the children of Israel became aware of the conspiracy against them that they naturally and spontaneously asked God for help.

But Nehemiah's prayer life was not the only aspect of his behavior that had affected these people. He was not a leader who only *told* people what to do but worked alongside of them, *showing* them what to do. From his example, they knew that prayer and hard work go together. Consequently, while they prayed, they "set up a guard" against their enemies "day and night" (4:9).

A New Set of Problems (Neh. 4:10-12)

Prayer and hard work—as we've seen in our previous chapter—was Nehemiah's spiritual formula for overcoming discouragement. But applying this formula to this new threat from their enemies did not work automatically for Israel. In fact, it created some new problems.

Physical and Psychological Fatigue (a Problem from Within)

Increased physical and psychological effort has an inevitable price tag, particularly when people are operating at maximum involvement. There were no fresh recruits, few coffee breaks and no long weekends or days off. For at least a month they had been exerting all the energy they could muster. And now they faced the threat of military attack. The people not only had to work all day at the wall, but some of them had to stand guard day *and* night. As a result fatigue began to set in.

Since Nehemiah had to assign some of the people to stand guard, the number of people who could work on the wall was reduced. Their work crew was further reduced when some had to guard at night. In addition, some of these people probably did double duty—working *both* day and night. Keep in mind also that by now all of the people were beginning to show signs of fatigue because of the tremendous effort they had already put out over the past several weeks.

Against this very pressurized backdrop, it is understandable why these people began to lose their physical and emotional momentum. Nehemiah reported on that problem in verse 10 when he wrote: "Thus in Judah it was said, 'The strength of the burden bearers is failing, yet there is much rubbish; and we ourselves are unable to rebuild the wall' " (4:10).

In the midst of total demoralization Nehemiah had succeeded in rallying these people to attack this project with unbelievable energy and motivation. Adrenalin had been flowing at a high level. But relentless pressure and hard work had taken its toll, as it always does. Those who were removing rubbish and dirt in order to make room for the builders were literally running out of steam. No doubt their task was the most physically demanding. And having to reduce the work force to face this new threat by assigning some to do guard duty only complicated the problem.

These people were also beginning to face the phenomenon that sets in when fatigue takes over: The task begins to look bigger than it really is. Little piles of dirt began to look like big piles of dirt. The last half of the walls looked much more difficult to complete than the first half of the walls. Many were ready to give up.

Threat of a Secret Attack (a Problem from Without)

But there were additional pressures. To complicate matters a number of reports began to come into the city by means of the Jews who lived outside of Jerusalem that their enemies were planning a secret attack. The message was very clear: "They will not know or see until we come among them, kill them, and put a stop to the work" (4:11). In other words the enemies of Israel were spreading the word among themselves that before the Jews knew anything had happened, it would all be over.

Nehemiah knew these reports did not represent idle gossip. In fact, on 10 different occasions he received a report, probably from different sources, and each time the message was basically the same: "They will come up against us from *every place* where you may turn" (4:12). In other words, Israel would not have a chance.

This information no doubt reduced further Israel's work force on the wall. Some of these people who lived outside Jerusalem would naturally succumb to the external pressure and stay home rather than go into the city to work and take a chance on being attacked and killed. And even if they were not killed, chances are, they concluded, they would be unable to return home to their families in case of attack. Only those totally committed to completing the task would have continued to take the risk of leaving home each day.

A New Strategy (Neh. 4:13-15)

Total commitment usually separates men from boys. When the "going gets tough," someone has said, "the tough get going." And there's no question on which side of the fence Nehemiah was on. His enemies' efforts at demoralizing him and the children of Israel simply did not work. Though he must have suffered unusual anxiety and stress, he did not allow a deteriorating situation to alter his objectives and his motivation. He knew God had led him to Jerusalem to rebuild the wall and he was not about to forsake his divinely appointed task. If God could change Artaxerxes' mind and grant him compassion before this man, He could certainly help His people ward off their enemies and finish the walls.

As morale continued to sink lower with each negative report from the Jews who lived outside the wall, Nehemiah knew he had to take action. He "stationed men in the lowest parts of the space behind the wall, the exposed places," and he stationed the people "in families with their swords, spears, and bows" (4:13).

This must have been a difficult decision for Nehemiah. To place *whole families* together—including women and children—put tremendous pressure on fathers particularly. In case of outright attack, they would have no choice but to stay and fight for and with their family members. In many respects it meant either living together or dying together. But Nehemiah knew it was the *only* decision he could make if they were to (1) survive and (2) succeed in rebuilding the walls.

Fear gripped these people. And Nehemiah knew it. He "*saw* their fear" (4:14). Consequently, he gathered the people together and charged them to face the situation courageously and to remember the One who was on their side. "Do not be afraid of them," he shouted. "Remember the Lord who is great and awesome" (4:14).

There are times we need to remember the *past*—what God has done for us when we've faced unusual pressures. This is particularly true when we are in the midst of a struggle or facing what seems to be an insurmountable problem. And this is what Nehemiah did, *first,* for his own encouragement, and *second,* for theirs. A number of months before, he had received a dismal report of what was happening in Jerusalem. Humanly speaking there was nothing he could do, except *pray* and *prepare himself* for an opportunity to ask the king for help. And in his prayer he acknowledged God as *Lord*—the *covenant* God of Israel. He also addressed Him as "the *great* and *awesome* God" (1:5). As we've seen, God answered that prayer, and Nehemiah knew God heard him because of His covenant with Israel.

Now he was facing another crisis, one so grave that from a human perspective it seemed that all he had *prayed for* and *worked for* was about to crumble and disintegrate. But Nehemiah remembered God's promises and how He had fulfilled these promises before. The challenge before him now was to help these people remember too!

"*Remember* the *Lord* who is *great* and *awesome!*" he proclaimed (4:14). In other words, "He's helped us before and He'll help us again! He is our covenant God! That's why I'm here! That's why the wall is half up! He is great! He is awesome! Let's continue to trust Him! Let's not give up now!"

Nehemiah's reminder was followed by a very difficult challenge. Simply remembering who God is and what He has promised seldom solves human predicaments. You must "fight," Nehemiah charged. And he reminded them that they were not simply fighting for themselves but for others—their "brothers," their "sons," their "daughters," their "wives"—and for the very places in which they lived—their own "houses."

Nehemiah's *reminder* plus his *challenge* worked, which gives us another one of his spiritual formulas for being a successful leader. In this instance he was helping his people face a very difficult crisis. *Prayer* and *hard work* had gotten them this far. But if they were to complete the task they needed to reflect on *who God is, what He had done for them in the past and then be prepared to lay down their lives for others to fulfill His will*.

And it worked! In fact, what happened is somewhat ironical. Nehemiah had received *information* regarding their enemies' plans to attack them secretly, which enabled the children of Israel to prepare for the attack. And once they were prepared, *information* got back to Israel's enemies that they were ready to face their attack. God in turn used this *counter-information* to frustrate their enemies' plans. Evidently they gave up the idea of attempting to stop the Jews through a *secret* attack. Otherwise Nehemiah could not have reported that "all of us returned to the wall, each one to his work" (4:15). This moral victory in turn spurred the Jews on and encouraged them to complete the task in spite of their physical and emotional exhaustion.

Once again we see Nehemiah's philosophy of life and ministry reflected in these events. Though he had worked hard at challenging the people and preparing them for a counterattack, he was quick to recognize that it was *God* who "had frustrated" their enemies' plans (4:15). Again we see the *human* and *divine* in intricate balance.

Three Important Lessons

What transpired in Jerusalem so many years ago yields some very practical and relevant lessons for Christians living in today's world. Let's look at at least three:

1. It is usually more difficult to complete the second half of a task than the first half. Once the Jews reached the *half-way point* in rebuilding the wall around Jerusalem, they faced a normal motivational problem. It seems that the second half of a task is always more difficult—especially a task that is exacting and intensely challenging.

Even though the score going into the locker room at half-time was the Jews 7 and the Samaritans 0, there were some dynamics in the second half that were unique. In the first half there's no question but that Nehemiah was a better quarterback. Sanballat, on the other hand, couldn't even get his team off the line of scrimmage.

But come the second half there was a problem. Nehemiah's team had worked their hearts out. They were physically and emotionally exhausted. But Sanballat was able to bring in fresh recruits and a whole new set of plays.

The analogy of course is clear. First, there is always a natural tendency for most of us to start strong as we attack challenging projects. But once we get into the thick of it, it is easy to lose momentum, particularly if we're putting out a lot of energy. Furthermore, once we get beyond the opening minutes (or hours) and settle into the step-by-step process, it's easy to lose sight of the goal. Excitement normally wanes when we get into the steady, day-by-day, nitty-gritty responsibilities of life.

Second, this tendency to let down is accentuated when we begin to grow weary. In fact, even as I write this sentence I'm aware of the fact that I've worked hard on this chapter most of the day. Furthermore, I'm physically and mentally tired. If it were not for a very important deadline early tomorrow morning, I'd put a period at this point and retire. But the fact is, I can't!

It takes unusual motivation to complete difficult tasks. Some people are surprised when I tell them that completing writing projects is one of my most difficult. Though I have written a number of books, I always have to generate a great deal of self-discipline and motivation to achieve these goals.

Speaking of projects, I'm reminded of the rather intricate dollhouse I began to build when my oldest daughter was in the *third* grade. Would you believe it is still sitting in the garage at home—*half-finished*? Incidentally, my daughter in now in her *third* year of college. (I still plan to complete the project—for my *grand*daughter.)

How many worthy projects are there in our Christian lives which we tackle enthusiastically, but never get beyond the half-way point? Remember! First, it's a natural tendency; second, fatigue and boredom will try to stop us every time; and third, Satan delights in incompleted tasks, particularly that are spiritually productive.

2. Fatigue can cause paranoia; so can uncertainty; and both together accentuate this tendency. What appears to be an achievable goal in the beginning stages of a project can become overwhelming and threatening when we get tired. This, of course, was part of Israel's problem. Because of *fatigue* the piles of rubbish near the wall seemed to be getting larger even though they were actually fewer and smaller.

Building on our earlier analogy of football, every good coach knows that a game is often won or lost on the basis of mental attitude. A team can beat itself by viewing their opponents as bigger and better than they are. On the other hand, an inferior team has beaten a stronger team by maintaining positive mental attitudes. And the facts are that when a team gets tired, the other team *always* looks bigger and better, even though they may not be.

Paranoid attitudes are also exaggerated by *uncertainty* which always accentuates our normal tendencies towards feelings of insecurity. And insecurity can cause our imaginations to run wild. And before long we have become negative thinkers and only see the dark side of life. This was part of the problem in Jerusalem. The *threat* of a secret attack only added fuel to their defeatist attitudes.

Some Christians have this problem living in the twentieth-century world. I've known some who have gotten involved in right-wing political and/or religious organizations that concentrate on the problems in our society. Before long, this is all they can think and talk about. They become obsessed with feelings of doom and gloom. They live in constant fear—fear that they're going to lose everything they own; fear that they are going to lose their freedoms; fear that they are going to suffer both physically and psychologically at the hands of the enemies of historical American values.

Needless to say, there are bad omens in our society. But Christians are to be able to live *above* these circumstances of life, and no matter what happens in our culture, we know that we are citizens of heaven. We have a home prepared for us that is not built with human hands. Christians of all people should be positive, not negative. Realistic? Yes! Pessimistic? No! The Bible teaches that we are to be people of *hope*.

Nehemiah faced head-on the problems that surrounded him. He did not hide his head in the sand. And he did not allow these problems to overwhelm him, sidetrack him, and eventually defeat him and his people. Together, and with the help of God, the Israelites rose above the problems of fatigue and uncertainty and succeeded in thwarting their enemies' efforts to destroy them.

3. Good leadership involves both modeling and exhortation. How beautifully we see this illustrated in the life of Nehemiah. What he *was*, the people *were becoming*. They *prayed* like him and they *worked* like him. But there came a time when Nehemiah had to remind the people who God was, what He had done for them, and that they should trust His promises. He also had to exhort them to fight to stand firm against their enemies, no matter what the price.

All of us as Christians need both good models *and* proper instruction and exhortation. And any good leader—whether father, mother, pastor, counselor, or teacher—knows that both are necessary. We must not neglect these elements in helping others to discover the will of God.

Life Response

1. What worthy projects do you have in process that are only half-finished—*and* at a standstill? Select the one that will be the most spiritually productive for others in your life—members of your family, your close Christian friends, or perhaps some non-Christian friends. Decide now that you are going to complete that project as soon as possible.

2. In what area of your life do you struggle most with

paranoid feelings? Could it be because of physical and emotional fatigue? To what extent are these feelings related to feelings of *uncertainty, inferiority,* and *insecurity*? Can you think of other reasons? Decide now how you might rise above these problems. You might:

☐ Talk with a close friend who will listen to you and give you good advice.

☐ Talk with a competent Christian counselor.

☐ Maybe you need to begin by taking a good vacation.

☐ If you are married, remember that both of you should be able to share your feelings without fear of rejection or retaliation.

3. As a Christian parent, pastor, teacher, or counselor, to what extent are you a good model of Christlike behavior as well as a good verbalizer?

REMEMBER: Words spoken that are not illustrated in life are often hollow and meaningless. In the words of Paul they become like "a noisy gong or a clanging cymbal" (1 Cor. 13:1). On the other hand, words spoken against the backdrop of a good model are meaningful and very difficult to ignore.

7

Nehemiah
Faces His Enemies Victoriously

Nehemiah 4:15-23

Nehemiah's strategy worked! When Israel's enemies discovered that their plan for a secret attack on Jerusalem was common knowledge and that the Jews had prepared themselves for such an attack, they were frustrated. In turn, this gave the children of Israel renewed courage and, in spite of their fatigue, their fears and their limited resources, they continued to rebuild the walls. However, they returned to their task far more cautiously.

"From That Day On" (Neh. 4:16-18)

Nehemiah records that "from that day on, . . . half of my servants carried on the work while half of them held the spears, the shields, the bows, and the breastplates" (4:16). And even those who carried on the work also carried weapons. Some of them transported materials, but used only one hand while they carried a weapon in the other (see 4:17). The rest of the work force who actually built the walls used both hands, but each carried a weapon at his side (see 4:18).

"The Sound of the Trumpet" (Neh. 4:19,20)

Nehemiah took another precaution. Since the workers were spread out all around the wall making them vulnerable to attack, he stationed a trumpeter next to him—a man who would follow him everywhere he went as he supervised the work. In case of an attack, the sound of the trumpet would rally the people to one place. And to make sure the people really knew Who was on their side, Nehemiah again emphasized the divine nature of their task. "Our *God* will fight for us," he said (4:20).

"From Dawn Until the Stars Appeared" (Neh. 4:21-23)

Though Nehemiah faced numerous problems before the wall was actually completed, the work went forward. The people worked diligently, from the crack of "dawn until the stars appeared" (4:21). Those living outside the city did not even return to their homes. Rather, they spent the night in Jerusalem, laboring by day and guarding by night. And even when they lay down to rest, they did not remove their clothes. Their weapons were constantly within arm's reach so that in a moment's notice they could be up and ready to confront their enemies[1] (see 4:23).

"With the Help of Our God" (Neh. 6:15,16)

Considering the problems and pressures they faced both externally and internally (there's more to come), there was no way to explain in purely human terms what happened. They actually completed the wall in an incredible 52 days (see 6:15). So amazing was this fact that when the enemies of Israel witnessed what had happened, "they lost their confidence" (6:16). And Nehemiah, as he consistently did throughout his historical record, made the reason for this reaction very clear:"For they recognized," he wrote, "that this work had been accomplished *with the help of our God*" (6:16).

Much earlier, when the Jews first began to "put their hands to the good work" (2:18), Nehemiah had confronted Sanballat, Tobiah and Geshem with this very truth. "The God of heaven will give us success" (2:20), he responded when they mocked and despised the children of Israel. But these words fell on deaf ears! They did not believe Nehemiah. But now—52 days later—they looked on in utter amazement. No doubt Nehemiah's earlier words came flashing back, ringing loudly in their ears. Their self-confidence disappeared as they realized there was only one way the children of Israel could have accomplished this task. Just as Nehemiah had proclaimed, the God of heaven indeed gave them success.

Charles Swindoll, writing about this grand culmination, states: "That has to be the most thrilling experience in the world—to watch God come to the rescue when you have been helpless. In the middle of the incessant assault of the enemy, in spite of the endless verbal barrage, the wall was built! While the enemy blasts, God builds."[2]

Who Are Your Enemies?

There are three special lessons we as Christians can learn from this passage.

1. We must be on constant guard against our greatest enemies. To complete the task God called them to, everyone in Israel had to be on guard against the enemies. With a sword in one hand and a trowel in the other, they worked day and night until they rebuilt the wall.

Most of our warfare as Christians is on a much different level than the people of God in the Old Testament. In fact, God has never called us to defend our faith with a literal sword. To justify a holy war on the basis of God's plans for Israel in the Old Testament is to miss completely the will of God for Christians. It is indeed a misapplication of biblical truth. "Our struggle," Paul wrote to the Ephesians, "is *not* against *flesh and blood,* but against the rulers, against the powers, against the world-forces of this darkness, against the *spiritual* forces of wickedness in the heavenly places" (Eph. 6:12).

In this New Testament passage Paul goes on to draw a unique parallel between a "flesh and blood" battle, and our "spiritual" battles. Using various pieces of armor and weapons ancient warriors used to protect themselves from their enemies, Paul made a direct application to the Christian's battle against Satan and his host of demons. "Put on the full *armor of God,*" Paul continued, "that you may be able to stand firm against the *schemes of the devil*" (6:11).

What are these *weapons* and what are the devil's *schemes*? Paul answers both of these questions clearly in this Ephesian passage.

First, gird "your loins with TRUTH" (Eph. 6:14). God is the author of *truth;* Satan is the "father of lies" (John 8:44). In fact, Jesus said, *"I am the . . . truth"* (John 14:6). There is no scheme so subtle as false information. And Satan uses it constantly against Christians. It is demoralizing and destructive, particularly when it is present in the Body of Christ.

One of the greatest ways to attack Satan and his evil schemes is to constantly search for truth. Remember that Satan's first evil tactic that plunged the whole world into sin was a lie. When Eve was first approached by Satan in the Garden of Eden, he tempted her to eat of the fruit of the tree in the midst of the garden. God had forbade that she do so. Satan told her, "You surely shall not die" (Gen. 3:4). This was the opposite of what God had told her (see Gen. 2:17). She believed Satan rather than God and consequently plunged the whole world into sin. From that point forward, all of us have found it easy to believe lies—particularly about other people. Therefore, Paul wrote, "Stand firm therefore, having girded your loins with *truth*" (Eph. 6:14).

Second, "Put on the breastplate of RIGHTEOUS-NESS" (Eph. 6:14). Not only is Satan the father of lies, but also of *all* wickedness and evil in the world. He has no greater desire than to lead Christians into sin. And he has been hard at work at this task ever since sin entered the world. Today he's working just as hard, permeating our culture and our own society. Have you ever noticed how much easier it is to gravitate towards sin than righteousness; towards immorality than morality; to be attracted to unholy behavior rather than holy behavior; to participate in ungodliness rather than godliness? This very natural tendency affirms the fact that the principle of sin is at work in our lives.

As Christians we must never leave off the breastplate of righteousness. Remember too that when we do sin, we find it easier to commit another sin. And before long, we are caught up in a web of unrighteousness. But it need not happen if we put on the "full armor of God." And that leads us to Paul's very next injunction.

Third, "Shod your feet with the preparation of the GOSPEL OF PEACE" (Eph. 6:15). There's some question as to what Paul means by this piece of armor. Personally, I believe it has to do with the good news of salvation in Jesus Christ. Writing to the Roman Christians, Paul said, "Therefore having been justified by faith, we have *peace* with God through our Lord Jesus Christ" (Rom. 5:1). As twentieth-century Christians we are living in the fullness of time. Jesus Christ has come. This is our hope and our message to others. And there is no greater defense against Satan than this great eternal truth. Through Christ we have peace with God. Our sins which separate us from God were paid for by Christ as He died on the cross. In fact, Paul had stated this already to the Ephesians earlier in this epistle. Speaking of their pre-conversion state, he said that they had "no hope" and were "without God in the world" (2:12). But by contrast, he reminded them of their blessed hope in Christ. "But now in Christ Jesus you . . . have been brought near by the blood of Christ. "For," wrote Paul, *"He Himself is our peace"* (2:13,14). Therefore, Paul later wrote to these same people, "Shod your feet with the preparation of the gospel of peace" (6:15).

Fourth, take "up the shield of FAITH" (Eph. 6:16). It is true that a Christian is *saved* by faith (see Eph. 2:8,9), but once we become Christians, we must also *walk* by faith (see Col. 2:6). It is this piece of armor, Paul wrote, with which we "will be able to extinguish all the flaming missiles of the evil one" (Eph. 6:16).

This process is illustrated graphically in Hebrews, chapter 11, a portion which we might call the "Hebrew Hall of Faith." There the author lists numerous individuals who conquered their enemies *by faith*. Moving into chapter 12, God makes it clear that these Old Testament greats are to be our example. Thus we read: "Therefore, since we have so great a cloud of witnesses surrounding us, let us also lay aside every encumbrance, and the sin which so easily entangles us, and let us run with endurance the race that is set before us, fixing our eyes on Jesus the author and perfecter *of faith*" (Heb. 12:1,2).

No matter what happens to us as Christians we must continue to believe God—to believe that He loves us, that He cares for us, that He wants to help us. Many years ago, John Yates captured the meaning of Paul's words in his lyrics, which were set to music by Ira Sankey.[3]

> Encamped along the hills of light,
> Ye Christian soldiers, rise,
> And press the battle ere the night
> Shall veil the glowing skies;

Against the foe in vales below
Let all our strength be hurled;
Faith is the victory, we know,
That overcomes the world.

My wife and I had the privilege of knowing the late Dr. Henrietta Mears, founder and director of Gospel Light Publications. She was influential in inspiring Bill Bright to found Campus Crusade, which was born in her home across from the UCLA campus. Billy Graham has stated that she had more influence in his life than any woman other than his mother. In fact, she was responsible for inspiring over 600 young men to enter the ministry. At one time it was stated that she probably led more people to Christ than any other person on the west coast.

Toward the end of her life she was asked what she would do differently if she had her life to live over again. Her response was immediate! "I would *believe* God more!"

Fifth, "Take the helmet of SALVATION" (Eph. 6:17). Satan is called the "accuser of the brethren." He delights in creating insecurity and fear, particularly regarding our personal relationship with Jesus Christ.

When I first became a Christian, my first temptation was to doubt my salvation. And for several years I fought a tremendous spiritual battle. When I felt good, I felt saved. When I felt bad, I felt lost. My security was in my *feelings*—not in the *facts* of the Word of God. This doubt was generated because I did not understand the gospel of Christ in its fullness. I did not understand my security in Jesus Christ, that He has promised to never leave us or forsake us. Once I understood that truth and believed it, I had peace in my heart. Even when I felt down, I still knew that God was the unchangeable One. His promises were true. He would never go back on His word. To stand effectively, I had to learn to "take the helmet of salvation."

Sixth, "Take . . . the sword of the Spirit, which is the WORD OF GOD" (Eph. 6:17). Here Paul becomes very specific. Our greatest defense against Satan is the Holy Scripture. In the Bible we have the complete written revelation of God. It even describes our enemy and his evil schemes in great detail. There's all we need to know regarding how to defeat him—which is graphically illustrated in the very passage before us.

Note also that Paul states that the Word of God is "the sword of the Spirit." One of the primary reasons God sent His Holy Spirit into this world and into the hearts of Christians was to reveal Himself through the Holy Scriptures. Jesus made this very clear to the apostles. Several times in John's Gospel He told His men that when He returned to heaven, the Father would send "the Spirit *of truth*" to counsel them and to help them (John 14:17; 16:13; see also 15:26). "He will *teach you* all things," Jesus said, "and *bring to your remembrance* all that I said to you" (John 14:26). And later Jesus was even more specific regarding the Holy Spirit's primary purpose in coming into the world. Preparing them for His departure, He said, "But when He, the *Spirit of truth*, comes, *He will guide you into all the truth* . . . and He will *disclose to you* what is to come" (John 16:13).

This promise was clearly fulfilled, for when Jesus Christ returned to heaven and the Holy Spirit came, it enabled the apostles particularly but not exclusively to speak forth the very words of God. It enabled the New Testament church to devote themselves to the *apostles' teaching* as the Holy Spirit revealed God's truth to them. Later, they recorded this truth for us in writing, which today comprises the New Testament documents, the full and complete revelation of God. Today the "Spirit of truth" has spoken and continues to speak through the Scriptures. In fact, it is the Word of God hidden in our hearts that the Holy Spirit, who also dwells in the hearts of all Christians, desires to use to enable us to defeat Satan. This is what Paul was referring to when he exhorted Christians "to stand firm against the schemes of the devil" (6:11) by taking "the sword of the Spirit, which is the word of God" (6:17).

Seventh, "PRAY at all times in the Spirit" (Eph. 6:18). With this final injunction regarding the way we as Christians can win spiritual warfare against Satan and his cohorts and come out on the victory side, Paul departs from his literal "weapons" and "armor" analogy and makes a very direct statement regarding prayer. It has always been and will always be the Christian's greatest weapon against Satan.

With this statement Paul emphasized *consistency* in prayer. "Pray *at all times,*" he wrote. And further, he said, pray "in the Spirit"; that is, pray according to the will of God. Herein Paul correlates prayer with his previous injunction, to take "the sword of the Spirit, which is the word of God" (v. 17). There's only one way for a twentieth-century Christian to be sure of God's will. There's only one way for us to be sure we are praying "in the Spirit." It is to pray according to what we know God has revealed to us. And that revelation has come from the Spirit of truth and is recorded in the Holy Scriptures. Consequently, the more we know of God's Word, the more we can pray "in the Spirit," knowing with certainty that we are praying according to the will of God.

Paul outlines before us therefore a very specific plan for being on constant guard against our enemies. This is one of the greatest lessons we can learn from Nehemiah's experience as he and his fellow Jews faced the enemies of Israel. But there are two more lessons that stand out boldly in this Old Testament story that correlates significantly with what we've just said.

2. As Christians we must stand together in our battles

against Satan. One of the greatest problems Nehemiah faced as the leader of Israel was to develop a means by which they could stand *together* in case of attack. "The work is great and extensive," he said, "and we are separated on the wall far from one another" (Neh. 4:19). Consequently, he appointed a man who would follow him everywhere he went and sound the trumpet in case of attack. "Rally to us there," he told the people (Neh. 4:20).

God never intended for Christians to face Satan alone. We need each other. There is *natural* strength in unity and mutual support and encouragement in doing things together. But when God's people are involved it is more than *natural*—it's also *supernatural*. It's the greatest means by which we can defeat Satan.

This was why Jesus prayed for unity among Christians (see John 17:21,23). And this is why Paul exhorted all of us as Christians to make every effort "to preserve the unity of the Spirit in the bond of peace" (Eph. 4:3). There is strength in unity, but we are always more vulnerable to defeat and failure when "we are separated . . . far from one another."

I know this is true in my own life. When I am out of harmony with other Christians—my wife, my children, or any of my brothers or sisters in Christ—I am far more vulnerable to Satan's attacks on my life. And remember! One of his greatest tools is not a direct Satanic attack, particularly in our culture. Rather, he subtly gets at us through our physical problems, and our psychological and spiritual weaknesses. And we all have these areas of vulnerability.

Again, let me emphasize that God never intended for any individual Christian to take on Satan alone. His army is too large, his power is too great and his knowledge too formidable. But *together*, as a Body in Christ, we *can* defeat him.

Unfortunately, as with many passages, we often

approach Paul's instructions to the Ephesians as merely personal. Rather, his instructions are to *all* the Christians in Ephesus. Though each Christian certainly must put on God's armor, the basic meaning of the passage is that we *as believers* are to wage war on Satan. *As Christians* we are to "be strong in the Lord" (Eph. 6:10). As a *Body of believers* we are to "put on the full armor of God" in order that we—as a Body—may be able to "stand firm against the schemes of the devil" (6:11). We're to look out for one another. We are to protect one another. We are to, as John said, "Lay down our lives" for one another (1 John 3:16). This is the secret to victory against Satan.

3. We should say with Nehemiah, "Our God will fight for us" (Neh. 4:20). It is true that God always places human responsibility on men. We must *follow* his instructions. We must *obey* His commands. We must *do* His will. But ultimately, God is the One who wins the victory—just as we've seen in every lesson that has emerged from our study of Nehemiah. And we see the same emphasis in Paul's letter to the Ephesians. We are to "be strong *in the Lord,* and in the strength of *His might*" (Eph. 6:10).

This is a necessary ingredient in the life of every Christian today if we're to be victorious over Satan. Our only problem is that we do not avail ourselves of God's resources, particularly in our contemporary culture. Christianity frequently becomes more of a convenience that we use only to meet our own needs. When it doesn't suit us, when Christ puts demands on our lives that we don't like, we find it easy to turn away from Him and take matters into our own hands.

One day at the Christian Booksellers Convention my wife and I had the privilege of meeting an African pastor who marked our lives in a unique way. His name is F. Kefa Sempangi. And when we read his book entitled *A Distant Grief,* the *real* story behind the martyrdom of Christians in

Uganda during Idi Amin's reign, the mark went deep into our souls. The pain was so deep that we shed tears. Our response was not so much related to these Christians' horrible experiences which often resulted in excruciating pain and death, though I must admit there were times as I read that I felt sick to my stomach. But the real impact upon our lives came as we became aware of our own apathy as Christians: our tendency to take God's love for granted, to become selfish, and to complain about the little things of life that don't always go our way.

Kefa himself, who was often the target of Amin's terrorist activities, eventually escaped from Uganda with his wife and daughter. Though he was willing to stay and continue to minister to the church that had swollen to a congregation of 14,000 people at the height of the persecution, he was ushered out of the country by others who were not so directly under attack as he was. How God delivered him from his enemies is in itself a miraculous story, for he was able to leave with only minutes to spare.

Through some previous contacts he was able to come to the United States where he continued his theological training. While here he set up a special foundation to help care for those in Uganda whose lives were spared—to care for their immediate needs, to educate orphans and to help whole families once again get on their feet economically.

But the part of the story that gripped me the most was Kefa's own testimony after arriving in the United States. He wrote:

> Our first semester passed quickly. Penina [his wife] gave birth to our son, Dawudi Babumba. In the fall I returned to my studies. It was then, in my second year, that I noticed the change that had come into my life. In Uganda, Penina and I read the Bible for hope and life. We read to hear God's promises, to hear His commands and obey them. There had been no time for argu-

ment and no time for religious discrepancies or doubts.

Now, in the security of a new life and with the reality of death fading from mind, I found myself reading Scripture to analyze texts and speculate about meaning. I came to enjoy abstract theological discussions with my fellow students and, while these discussions were intellectually refreshing, it wasn't long before our fellowship revolved around ideas rather than the work of God in our lives. It was not the blood of Jesus Christ that gave us unity, but our agreement on doctrinal issues. We came together not for confession and forgiveness but for debate.

The biggest change came to my prayer life. In Uganda I had prayed with a deep sense of urgency. I refused to leave my knees until I was certain I had been in the presence of the resurrected Christ. It was not just the gift I needed. I needed to see the Giver. I needed to know that the God of orphans and widows, the God of the helpless, heard my prayers. Now, after a year in Philadelphia, the urgency was gone. When I prayed publicly I was more concerned to be theologically correct than to be in God's presence. Even in private my prayers were no longer the helpless cries of a child. They were spiritual tranquilizers, thoughts that made no contact with anything outside themselves. More and more, I found myself coming to God with vague requests for gifts I did not expect.

One night, I said my prayers in a routine fashion

and was about to rise from my knees when I heard the convicting voice of the Holy Spirit.

"Kefa, who were you praying for? What is it you wanted? I used to hear the names of children in your prayers, the names of friends and relatives. You prayed for Okelo and Topista, for Dr. K. and Ali, for Nakazi and your father. Now you pray for 'the orphans,' for 'the church' and your 'fellow refugees.' Which refugees, Kefa? Which believers? Which orphans? Who are these people and what is it you want for them?"

It was a sharp rebuke. As I fell again to my knees and asked for forgiveness for my sin of unbelief, I knew that it was not just my prayers that had suffered. It was not just a bad memory that caused names to vanish from my mind and turned those closest to me into abstractions. God Himself had become a distant figure. He had become a subject of debate, an abstract category. I no longer prayed to Him as a living Father but as an impersonal being who did not mind my inattention and unbelief.

From that night on, my prayers became specific. I prayed for real people, with real needs. And it was not long before, once again, these needs became the means by which I came face to face with the living God.[4]

For those of us living in the United States, the lesson is clear. How much does God really mean to us? How real is He? How meaningful is our Christian experience? How easy it is to be lulled to sleep by the comforts of life, the blessings of life, the freedoms of life. And before long, we operate like mechanical Christians, without hearts of compassion and without a sense of urgency. If Kefa found it easy to be lulled into a state of complacency in only a year, after experiencing years of persecution and attacks on his own life, how easy it is for us who know nothing of what it means to suffer because of those who hate us and the Christ we serve!

Don't misunderstand! I don't believe we should feel *bad* because God has blessed us! But I believe we ought to feel bad if we're not thankful. I believe we should feel bad *if* we're ungrateful. I believe we should feel bad *if* we're selfish and unwilling to share and to help others. I believe we should feel bad *if* we are only academic followers of Jesus Christ.

The Scriptures are clear. God wants us to be Christians who see beyond our affluence, our luxuries, our freedoms and see a God who cares for us and who cares for others. He wants us to see Himself, a God who wants to fight for us and help us not to become enmeshed in a materialistic and immoral world that can dull our sensitivities to His Word and the things of the Spirit!

Life Response

The following questions will help you apply these lessons specifically to your own life. Be honest!

1. To what extent are you constantly standing guard against Satan's subtle attacks on your life? What is your greatest need? Use the following checklist:

☐ a. I need to gird my loins with *truth*

☐ b. I need to put on the breastplate of *righteousness*

☐ c. I need to shod my feet with the preparation of the *gospel of peace*

☐ d. I need to take the shield of *faith*

☐ e. I need to put on the helmet of *salvation*

☐ f. I need to take the sword of the Spirit which is the *Word of God*

☐ g. I need to *pray* at all times in the Spirit

2. To what extent are you making *every effort* to maintain the unity of the Spirit in the bond of peace? Think of specific things you can do to contribute to unity rather than disunity. What can you do immediately?

3. To what extent is your Christianity man-centered rather than God-centered? Remember, God wants to fight for us no matter what our problems—be it selfishness, ungratefulness, half-hearted commitment to Jesus Christ, etc.

Notes

1. The actual meaning of chapter 4, verse 23 is vague in the Hebrew text. C.F. Keil translates, "And each laid his weapon on the right, viz. When he laid himself down at night to rest in his clothes, to be ready for fighting at the first signal from the watch." *Biblical Commentary on the Old Testament*, the books of Ezra, Nehemiah, Esther, p. 207. Though variously translated, the main point is clear both textually and contextually. They were ready to fight day and night.

2. Charles R. Swindoll, *Hand Me Another Brick* (Nashville: Thomas Nelson, Inc. Publishers, 1978), p. 137.

3. John H. Yates, "Faith Is the Victory." Public domain.

4. F. Kefa Sempangi, *A Distant Grief* (Ventura, CA: Regal Books, 1979), pp. 179,180.

8

Nehemiah
Faces Internal Problems

Nehemiah 5:1-13

To this point in this Old Testament story, Nehemiah's challenges as a spiritual leader focus primarily on those *outside* of Israel. But before the walls were finally rebuilt, he encountered one of the most difficult and intense problems every spiritual leader has to face—problems *within*. For Nehemiah, those problems centered not on Sanballat or Tobiah or Geshem but around his own people, Israel. And the intensity of the problems is reflected by the fact that "there was a great *outcry* of the people and of their wives against their Jewish brothers" (Neh. 5:1). What were these problems that created such emotional pain in Israel?

The Internal Problems (Neh. 5:1-5)

First, among some there was a food shortage. "We,

our sons and our daughters, are many," they complained; "therefore let us get grain that we may eat and live" (Neh. 5:2).

Second, others had enough to eat but they were mortgaging their fields, their vineyards and their homes in order to buy food (see 5:3).

Third, still others, in order to keep their property, had to borrow money from their Jewish brothers to pay taxes to King Artaxerxes (see 5:4). This problem, however, was compounded by the fact that they were charged exorbitant interest rates by their own Jewish brothers.

And this led to a fourth problem. If their crops failed—as they did because of famine—their creditors would take away their property and sell their children into slavery (see 5:5). This, of course, left them in a hopeless state. There was no way out. "We are *helpless*," they cried, "because our fields and vineyards belong to others" (5:5).

There are several reasons why these problems existed. First, many of the people dedicated themselves completely to rebuilding the walls. While in the process they ran out of personal resources. To complicate matters they were experiencing a famine (see 5:3) and were unable to produce enough food to sustain them. And to make matters exceedingly worse, the rich in Israel were taking advantage of the poor—a phenomenon that has happened consistently throughout the history of the world.

Another reason, not specifically mentioned by Nehemiah, probably involved stealing and robbery. The small farms that belonged to the children of Israel were always considered fair game by their enemies. At times, after the farmers had waited patiently for harvest time, rebel bands would descend on their fields and vineyards and strip them clean. In view of the psychological warfare already waged against Israel, it doesn't take much imagination to figure out that their enemies were contributing to their internal problems.

All of these difficulties created an internal crisis in Israel. And of course it meant double trouble for Nehemiah. Not only were the enemies of Israel a constant threat to their security and state of well-being, but now many in Israel were actually taking advantage of others. Morale, which was already at an all-time low because of external pressures, physical exhaustion and fear, took another plunge because of these internal difficulties.

Nehemiah's Initial Response

Any one of us who might be standing in Nehemiah's shoes can predict his reactions. He became "very angry." In many respects this must have been the final blow that disturbed his emotional equilibrium. After all, he was a human being. When everyone else in Israel had been ready to give up the ship, he had stood firm against impossible odds, exhorting them to trust God and not to give up. When morale had hit rock bottom he didn't dare show signs of personal fatigue and discouragement. If he had, all of their initial efforts would have literally crumbled before their very eyes. Once again Israel would have gone down in defeat as they had so many times before.

But now, internal strife! Fathers and mothers and children going hungry! Families losing their properties and sources of income. Sons and daughters being sold into slavery! And worst of all, brothers taking advantage of brothers in the midst of this crisis situation! It was too much! "Then I was *very angry*," reports Nehemiah, "when I heard their outcry and these words" (5:6).

But Nehemiah's anger was prompted by more than low emotional tolerance. Though it is logical and understandable to conclude that this must have been a factor, it was not the primary reason. Nehemiah's anger was directed at selfishness, greed and insensitivity. People were hurting and suffering—and those who should have been the most compassionate were those most guilty of exploitation. Nehemiah's anger was *righteous* anger.

At this juncture we can learn a great lesson from Nehemiah. In spite of his intense emotional state—remember that he was not just angry, but *very* angry—he did not take immediate action. Rather, we read, "I consulted with myself" (5:7).

The Hebrew word translated "consult" literally means "to give oneself advice" or to "counsel oneself." Nehemiah got distance on the problem, which enabled him to cool down, to gather all the facts, to get them in proper perspective and *then* to decided on a course of action.

It is also helpful at this point to enter into the process with Nehemiah and focus on the facts. Not only were some of the elite in Israel violating the *spirit* of the Mosaic law, but also the literal *letter* of the law. Many years earlier God had spoken to Israel from Mount Sinai and said, "If you lend money to My people, to the *poor* among you, you are not to act as a creditor to him; you shall not charge him interest" (Exod. 22:25).

Furthermore, no Jew was *ever* to enslave another Jew. This was clear from another Old Testament passage describing God's law to Israel and which interrelates the two points at which some in Israel were violating God's specific instructions. We read: "Now in case a countryman of yours becomes poor and his means with regard to you falter, [which describes specifically what had happened to some of the Jews in Nehemiah's days], then you are to sustain him, like a stranger or a sojourner, that he may live with you. Do not take usurious interest from him, but revere your God, that your countryman may live with you. . . . And if a countryman of yours becomes so poor with regard to you that he sells himself to you, you shall not subject him to a slave's service. He shall be with you as a hired man, as if he were a sojourner with you, until the year of jubilee. He shall then go out from you, he and his sons with him, and shall go back to his family, that he may return to the property of his forefathers" (Lev. 25:35,36,39-41).

Nehemiah's anger then was vented, not just at people in Israel who were exploiting others, but at a violation of God's instructions. While they were praying to God for help and assistance in rebuilding the wall (which God was granting freely, and without "interest," we might add), they were ignoring His commands. Their exploitation not only involved their fellow Jews, but their God.

Nehemiah's Specific Actions (Neh. 5:7-11)

With this perspective Nehemiah confronted the situation head-on. As a spiritual leader in Israel he had no choice if he wanted to be in the will of God himself. God had called him, not only to rebuild the walls of Jerusalem, but to make sure the people obeyed His laws.

First, Nehemiah *rebuked* those who were violating God's commands. He "contended with the nobles and the rulers and said to them, 'You are exacting usury, each from his brother!'" (5:7). And notice that what was happening in Israel was such a *public* issue that Nehemiah had to deal with it *publicly*. He reports that he "held a *great assembly* against them" (5:7).

Second, Nehemiah points out the inconsistency of their behavior compared with what he and others in exile had done personally to help their brothers. "We according to our ability have redeemed our Jewish brothers who were sold to the nations; now would you even sell your brothers that they may be sold to us?" (5:8). In other words, Nehemiah is saying, "We are paying money out of our own pockets to free our people from their pagan masters, and you come along and sell them again so we have to redeem them a second time—and this time from you."

But Nehemiah did not stop at this point. Right is right and wrong is wrong. God's name and reputation were at stake. Sin must be dealt with. This immoral and unethical behavior must be changed so they would not bring reproach on the One who had delivered them from both Egyptian bondage and Babylonian captivity. Consequently, Nehemiah exhorted, "The thing which you are doing is not good; should you not walk in the fear of our God because of the reproach of the nations, our enemies?" (5:9).

Nehemiah's final point and appeal was intensely personal. He referred to his own personal example and others who were helping those in need. "Look," he said. "My brothers and I and our servants are actually lending them money and grain—and without interest. Won't you do the same?" (see 5:10). In other words, Nehemiah was not asking these people to do something he was not exemplifying in his own life. This character trait in itself reveals why Nehemiah was such an outstanding spiritual leader and why he got such significant results.

In this Old Testament narrative we move now to the bottom line, Nehemiah's specific exhortations and personal appeals. He asked those guilty of exploitation to return what they had taken from the poor—"their fields, their vineyards, their olive groves, and their houses"—plus the interest they were "exacting from them" (5:11). Many years later Jesus told His disciples that if they indeed loved Him they would obey Him (see John 15:10). And in this Old Testament setting centuries earlier, Nehemiah was telling God's people the same thing. "If you really love God and appreciate what He's done for you, you'll obey His laws and have compassion on those who are not as fortunate as you are."

There's one other point in Nehemiah's exhortation that needs emphasis. There's a sense of urgency and immediacy in Nehemiah's statements. He did not ask them to go home and think about what they had done and consider how they might rectify the situation. He didn't even ask them to spend time in prayer. Rather, he said, "Please, give back to them this *very day* their fields, their vineyards, ..." In other words, "Deal with your sin now! Make restitution *now!* Don't wait, even until tomorrow!"

The People's Response (Neh. 5:12,13).

Again, Nehemiah's point was very clear. He pulled no spiritual punches. His appeals were on target. Though it may appear he went for the *jugular vein,* in actuality he went for the *heart,* which again sets him off as a mature spiritual leader. And you can imagine the joy and happiness that must have surged through his psychological veins when the people responded to his exhortations. What remained of his initial anger must have been replaced with very positive emotions. "We will give it back and will require nothing from them," they responded; "we will do *exactly* as you say" (5:12).

This may have been more than Nehemiah had hoped for. But there's no doubt this was what he had prayed for. But he also knew that words are cheap and easy to utter on the spur of the moment and particularly under public pressure. Consequently, he asked them to take another step—to publicly take an oath in the presence of the spiritual leaders in Israel indicating they would actually do what they said they would do (see 5:12).

And to seal that oath, he graphically visualized for them the grave consequences that could come to them if they lied to God. He used his garment as a visual demonstration, shaking it out. "Thus may God shake out every man from his house and from his possessions who does not fulfill this promise; even thus may he be shaken out and emptied" (5:13).

Biblical Lessons for Twentieth-Century Living

In studying this passage it is obvious there are some very practical and dynamic lessons that stand out in bold type. We've already alluded to these as we've looked at the internal problems faced and how Nehemiah resolved them. Let's be more specific, however.

1. Internal problems are inevitable. Wherever you have people in close association, even Christian people, you inevitably experience internal problems. There is no perfect family and no perfect church. Some people don't really seem to believe that. For example, I've met people who actually seem to be looking for the perfect church. I have a standard response to their request: "Our church is certainly not perfect because I'm there. Furthermore, you will add to the imperfection if you join us."

On the other hand, it is God's will that internal problems be minimal. He has given us His Word, and if we constantly obey His Word, we can defeat Satan's attempts to interfere in our human relationships.

This is illustrated well in Nehemiah's account regarding the internal struggles in Israel. Had they obeyed God's laws in the first place, they would not have created the internal turmoil that existed. Furthermore, when they obeyed God's law, the problem was resolved. As Christians we have at our disposal all the divine resources we need to face internal problems and resolve them. We simply need to obey what God says. For example, following are some very important biblical guidelines from Ephesians 4:

• "Walk in a manner worthy of the calling with which you have been called, with all humility and gentleness, with patience, showing forbearance to one another in love" (4:1,2).
• "[Be] diligent to preserve the unity of the Spirit in the bond of peace" (4:3).
• "[Lay] aside falsehood, speak truth, each one of you, with his neighbor, for we are members of one another" (4:25).

• "Be angry, and yet do not sin; do not let the sun go down on your anger, and do not give the devil an opportunity" (4:26,27).

• "Let him who steals steal no longer; but rather let him labor, performing with his own hands what is good, in order that he may have something to share with him who has need" (4:28).

• "Let no unwholesome word proceed from your mouth, but only such a word as is good for edification according to the need of the moment, that it may give grace to those who hear" (4:29).

• "Let all bitterness and wrath and anger and clamor and slander be put away from you, along with all malice" (4:31).

• "Be kind to one another, tender-hearted, forgiving each other" (4:32).

Jesus Christ Himself adds another important dimension and guideline for dealing with personal problems that often create internal strife. He said: "And if your brother sins [against you], go and reprove him in private; if he listens to you, you have won your brother. But if he does not listen to you, take one or two more with you, so that by the mouth of two or three witnesses every fact may be confirmed. And if he refuses to listen to them, tell it to the church [a larger assembly]; and if he refuses to listen even to the church, let him be to you as a Gentile and a tax-gatherer" (Matt. 18:15-17).

If this guideline alone, which was given by Jesus Christ, were carefully followed by the average Christian, there would be few internal problems that could not be solved quickly, both within the family and within the church.

2. *Internal problems usually cause negative emotions.* Negative emotions, particularly anger, must be handled in a biblical way or we will intensify and multiply

internal problems. In Nehemiah's situation, what happened first of all created deep distress among the people who were being exploited and hurt. It always works that way. Secondly, it created intense anger in Nehemiah.

As Christians we must be prepared to handle these negative emotions constructively and biblically. Nehemiah of course illustrates beautifully with his own life how to handle intense anger.

First, we must understand the nature of our anger. Is it based on facts? Do I understand those facts? Am I reacting because I'm simply hurt or threatened, or is there justifiable reason for my anger?

Second, to understand anger we need time to reflect and gain perspective before we take action. Putting it another way, we need to get some distance on the problem. Time has a way of clearing away emotional fog and creating more objective thinking.

Nehemiah's anger of course *was* justified. But even then he gained perspective before taking action. He reflected and thought about the matter. No doubt, he reviewed the Mosaic law to make sure he had God's perspective on the problem as well as his own.

As I reflect on my own life and the times I have gotten angry, I really can't remember too many times when it compares with Nehemiah's experience. In most instances, I'm simply hurt or feel rejected. This does not mean that the anger I feel is necessarily wrong or sinful, unless it grows out of purely selfish attitudes and actions. But how I handle anger does reflect righteousness or unrighteousness.

The best way to handle personal anger, particularly in close relationships, is to sensitively and nondestructively share our feelings with those causing the anger. We should not repress it or brood. I believe this is what Paul meant in the Ephesian passage when he said, "Be angry, and yet do not sin; do not let the sun go down on your anger" (4:26). If you do, Paul implies, you'll "give the devil an opportunity" (4:27).

Nehemiah's anger, however, was not provoked by the nitty-gritty relationships in life. He was dealing with social injustice. The elite in Israel were engaging in flagrant sin by violating very clear and direct statements and commands from God. In this sense, Nehemiah was very righteous in his anger. But even then, he gained perspective. He did not act on impulse. He made sure he had God's viewpoint on the problem.

Impulsive anger, even though it may be "righteous" will get us into trouble if we're not careful. Furthermore, it will not bring the intended results. I remember attending a Cowboy/Cardinal football game in Texas Stadium several years ago with my family. Seated next to me was my young son, and next to him one of my daughters and my wife. Directly in front of me was a man who was imbibing too much alcohol.

As the game progressed, he got more hostile and violent in his language. Furthermore, he made a point of standing up every time the Cowboys advanced the ball— which blocked my view—and in the process shouted obscenities at a Cardinal fan who was sitting directly behind me.

Needless to say, my anger level was rising by degrees. First, I was upset because of my family members who had to sit and listen to such language coming from a grown man. Second, though I'm an ardent Cowboy fan, I was embarrassed for the Cardinal fan. Third, he was just plain blocking my vision, and that's a no-no when I go to Texas Stadium.

Unfortunately, I tried to take matters into my own hands without consulting myself or anybody else—including the Lord. As could be predicted, my communication wasn't too well received, which caused him to stand up and attempt to knock my block off. I quickly stood up to protect myself and to a casual observer it looked as if I may even have initiated the encounter.

The stadium guard, who saw what was happening, didn't have a correct perspective on the problem. Consequently, I was told in no uncertain terms along with the other "gentleman" that if I didn't straighten up, we'd both be locked up.

Incidentally, it would have really looked neat in the *Dallas Morning News* the next morning to read the following: "Pastor/Seminary Professor Arrested in Texas Stadium for Engaging in a Drunken Brawl." Fortunately, people around me came to my rescue and explained the situation to the guard. But as I reflected on that experience, I see now how I could have handled the situation much differently and with less embarrassing results for me and my whole family. (You should have seen the look on my young son's face when all of this was happening.) Had I "consulted with myself," as I did later, I would have simply reported the situation to the proper authorities. They would have handled the problem, and much less emotionally than I.

In summary, internal problems always cause negative emotions—particularly anger—but we must handle this anger in a biblical way or we will intensify and multiply the problem. This is particularly true in a group of people meeting together for public discussion and action. There's no quicker way to lose respect than to lose control in a larger social setting.

3. Solving problems requires example. When dealing with people who are creating internal problems, we must exemplify in our own lives the exhortations and appeals we are issuing. This was one very important reason why Nehemiah was a very successful spiritual leader. In this instance, he used his personal behavior toward the poor to illustrate correct actions in obedience to God's laws. In fact, as a spiritual leader he seemingly exemplified with his own life *everything* he asked others to do. When he asked them to rebuild the walls, he worked alongside them. And when he asked them to pray, he prayed. When he asked them to trust God, he trusted God. When he asked them to work night and day, he also worked night and day. And in this instance, when he asked them to help the poor, he illustrated that he too was helping the poor.

This principle is very important in all we do as Christians. As parents, for example, we must visualize and dramatize for our children our expectations from them. "Do as I say and not as I do" is a destructive philosophy of leadership in the home and in the church.

In my own ministry I have set up this principle of exemplification as a biblical goal. Though I don't always live up to it as I should, I try, as a spiritual leader, never to ask people to do something I am not willing to do myself. If I expect people to live a consistent Christian life, I must live a consistent Christian life. If I encourage people to share their faith with non-Christians, I must be sharing my faith with non-Christians. If I exhort people to pray for others, I too must pray for others. If I ask people to be good stewards of God's gifts and talents, I must be a good steward of God's gifts and talents to me. If I ask people to give sacrificially to a special project, I must also give sacrificially to that project. In fact, as a Christian leader, I find it very difficult to ask people to do anything I have not done myself. Though I do not always measure up as I would like—God knows I fail at some points—I find it also puts realistic guidelines on what I actually ask people to do. It keeps me out of the ivory tower of theology and in the workshop of everyday life.

Exemplification is indeed basic in being an effective pastor, parent, or person. Nehemiah illustrates it graphically in his leadership of Israel. And Paul exemplified it in his own life in the New Testament church. Consequently, he wrote to the Corinthians: "Be imitators of me, just as I also am of Christ" (1 Cor. 11:1). And on another occasion he wrote to the Thessalonians: "You are witnesses, and so is God, how devoutly and uprightly and blamelessly we behaved toward you believers" (1 Thess. 2:10). What a practical goal this is for twentieth-century Christians!

Life Response

Using the following checklist, isolate at least *one area* in your Christian life that needs attention and determine with God's help that you are going to do God's will as soon as possible.

In view of Paul's injunctions in Ephesians 4, what can I do to resolve any relational problems that I have?

☐ With my marital partner
☐ With my children
☐ With my parents
☐ With my fellow Christians

Do I follow Nehemiah's example in handling my negative emotions constructively?

☐ Toward my marital partner
☐ Toward my children
☐ Toward my parents
☐ Toward my fellow Christians

Do I exemplify in my own life what I except and ask of others?

☐ From my marital partner
☐ From my children
☐ From my parents
☐ From my fellow Christians

9

Nehemiah's
Perspective on Promotion

Nehemiah 5:14-9

Nehemiah, probably more than any other Old Testament character, demonstrates strength of character in times of advancement as well as in days of adversity. And the passage before us illustrates this fact.

Nehemiah Appointed as Governor

At some point during the process of rebuilding the walls of Jerusalem, Nehemiah was appointed governor of Jerusalem. Within the confines of Israel at that moment in their history, there was no higher position of leadership.

Later, as Nehemiah wrote his historical account of his years in Jerusalem, he inserted a paragraph describing his perspective on that promotion. His rationale for inserting this descriptive paragraph at this point in his narrative was prompted by the events he described in the previous paragraph (see Neh. 5:1-13). Sometime during the rebuilding of the wall, it came to Nehemiah's attention that the elite of Israel were selfishly exploiting the poor. Nehemiah faced the problem head-on and resolved it. In the process he appealed to the offenders on the basis of his own exemplary behavior in showing concern for the poor.

This specific event during his early days as leader in Israel caused him to jump ahead in this historical account and talk briefly about his 12-year experience as governor of Jerusalem. In other words, the passage before us is definitely sequential, but describes a 12-year period of time.

Nehemiah Did Not Use His Privileges

Promotion usually brings privileges. And one of the privileges given to Nehemiah as governor was a food allowance. Using twentieth-century nomenclature, he had an expense account. However, even though he was entitled to a certain amount of food to do official entertaining, he did not take advantage of what was rightfully his. "Moreover," he wrote, "from the day that I was appointed to be their governor in the land of Judah, from the twentieth year to the thirty-second year of King Artaxerxes, for twelve years, neither I nor my kinsmen have eaten the governor's food allowance" (Neh. 5:14).

This did not mean that Nehemiah did not have a need to entertain. Even though he did not use his food allowance, he still fed regularly 150 Jews at his own table—men and officials who were part of his gubernatorial staff. In addition, he entertained on a regular basis visiting dignitaries from the nations surrounding Israel (see 5:17).

For most of us it is very difficult to imagine the amount of food this took every day. Consequently, Nehemiah recorded for us exactly how much—one ox, six sheep, and an unspecified number of birds. And then, every 10 days, Nehemiah abundantly supplied everyone with "all sorts of wine" (5:18). In all the years Nehemiah served as governor, he did not use his *legitimate* food allowance to pay for this food. In other words, it came out of his own personal resources.

"Why?" you ask. "Didn't he deserve to use his expense account?" The answer of course is yes. It would have been very legitimate. But Nehemiah had his reasons, which we'll look at a little later. But first, let's look at two other observations regarding his personal example as governor.

Nehemiah Did Not Abuse His Privileges

Promotion usually not only provides people with certain legitimate privileges, but also provides unique opportunities to take advantage of those privileges. Nehemiah made it clear in his narrative that governors before him had done that very thing. They "laid burdens on the people," he wrote, "and took from them bread and wine besides forty shekels of silver." And, he added, "even their servants domineered the people" (5:15).

All of the specifics Nehemiah had in mind are not totally clear in verse 15. But one thing is *very* clear. Former governors of Jerusalem went *beyond* their rightful privileges. They took advantage of their position of power and used it to pad their own pockets. Their profit-sharing scheme involved their servants who became primarily responsible to collect both money and produce from the people.

This, of course, was an insidious system. The more food and money the servants could bring into the governor's coffers, the bigger their own personal cut. Understandably, this would lead to incredible exploitation.

This kind of problem is not new. We see frequent reference to it in the Gospels. For example, Zacchaeus is identified as a "*chief* tax-gatherer." He is also specifically identified as being very rich (see Luke 19:2). The reason for his enormous wealth was well known. The more he could collect from the people, the more he could keep for himself.

When Zaccheus came face to face with Jesus Christ and His way of life, he immediately acknowledged his unethical behavior and was also willing to make right what he had done wrong. He said, "Behold, Lord, half of my possessions I will give to the poor, and if I have defrauded anyone of anything, I will give back four times as much" (Luke 19:8).

Matthew (also called Levi), who became one of the 12 apostles, was also a tax collector. After he decided to follow Christ, he planned a large banquet in his home and invited a great number of his fellow tax collectors to come and meet Jesus.

The reaction of the religious leaders in Israel is very revealing. Speaking to Jesus and the other disciples, they asked, "Why do you eat and drink with the tax-gatherers *and sinners*?" (Luke 5:30). In their minds the two were synonymous. And in his response Jesus did not deny this reality, "It is not those who are well who need a physician, but those who are sick. I have not come to call righteous men but sinners to repentance" (Luke 5:31,32).

In Nehemiah's day there were different factors politically, but in essence the dynamics were the same. Those in power often exploited people through a very similar system. And thus Nehemiah reported that governors before him "laid burdens on the people" and "even their servants domineered the people" (Neh. 5:15). In other words they *abused* their privileges.

Nehemiah Did Not Become Guilty of a Conflict of Interest

This phenomenon is of course an extension of our previous observation. Abuse of privilege often involves conflicting interest.

It would have been very easy for Nehemiah to fall into this trap. Once appointed governor, he could have concentrated on lending people money to pay their taxes, having them use their land as collateral. And then, when they could not pay back what they had borrowed, he could have applied the standards of the world and taken back their land. He, along with the other elite people in Judah, could have exploited the poor.

This was what Nehemiah meant when he wrote, "We did not buy any land." Rather, he said, "I also applied myself to the work on the wall . . . and all my servants were gathered there for the work" (5:16). In other words, Nehemiah could have used his position as governor to become a man of even greater wealth and power. Under the guise of helping people (lending them money), he could eventually have taken as his own everything they possessed. He could have literally made them his personal slaves.

To do so, of course, would have been in direct violation of the law of God. However, since governors before him had behaved in this manner, and in view of the fact that many of the elite in Israel were already participating in such activities, he could easily have followed suit. But Nehemiah never lost sight of God's calling in his life. He was in Jerusalem to help the people, not to exploit them. He was there to exemplify the law of God, not to violate it. He was there to rebuild the wall, not to build a personal empire.

Nehemiah's Motivation as Governor

What motivated Nehemiah, not only to avoid abusing his privileges as governor, but also to avoid using the privileges that were legitimately his?

First, Nehemiah did not abuse his privileges as governor because he feared God (5:15). He knew it would be wrong, that it would be a violation of the law of God. This is why he became so furious at the nobles and rulers in Israel who were exploiting the poor by lending them money, charging them interest, confiscating their land and then enslaving them when they had nothing left to pay off their debts. Nehemiah was committed to obeying God and doing His will. He could not and would not in good conscience abuse his privileges as governor.

Second, Nehemiah did not use the privileges that were legitimately his because he was sensitive to people's needs. This he also made clear in his historical account. Speaking of the amount of food he served regularly, he wrote: "Yet for all this I did not demand the governor's food allowance, *because the servitude was heavy on this people*" (5:18).

Even though the people themselves realized that Nehemiah had special privileges as their governor and that he was responsible to feed his staff of people, he did not use this privilege because of the extensive burden the people themselves were already bearing. For years they had been struggling against their enemies. Their morale was at an all-time low. They barely had enough food to feed themselves and at times they went hungry. And in the midst of all of these difficulties they were trying to accomplish the impossible—to rebuild the walls of Jerusalem. Under these circumstances Nehemiah decided to give up his personal privileges and bear the burden with the people. If they were willing to sacrifice their own personal resources and their own personal comforts to achieve God's will, he decided to remove the burden from them of caring for the food that he and his staff needed. Rather, Nehemiah picked up the tab himself.

Third, Nehemiah's noble actions as governor were motivated by the fact that he desired God's special blessing on his life. "Remember me, O my God, for good," he wrote, "according to all that I have done for this people" (5:19; see also 13:14,22,31).

Nehemiah did not hesitate to let everyone know that part of his motivation for doing what was right as a leader in Israel was that he wanted God to bless him. He remembered well that God had promised Israel "blessings" if they obeyed him but a "curse" if they did not (see Deut. 28:1-68). The Babylonian captivity, which resulted from Israel's disobedience, was still very fresh in his mind. And no doubt his memory went back even further, to what God had said to Joshua as he was about ready to lead the children of Israel into the Promised Land. "Be careful to do according to all the law which Moses My servant commanded you; *do not turn from it to the right* or to the left, *so that you may have success* wherever you go. This book of the law shall not depart from your mouth [that is, you should teach it consistently], but you shall meditate on it day and night, so that you may be careful *to do according to all that is written in it; for then you will make your way prosperous, and then you will have success*" (Josh. 1:7,8).

A Twentieth-Century Perspective on Promotion

Nehemiah's experience and example as governor of Jerusalem speaks clearly to every Christian, but particularly to those of us who are involved in the workaday world. As we progress along the continuum of time, and especially as we do our jobs well, we face the reality of increased responsibilities and promotions. It is a part of our social and economic system, and we certainly wouldn't want it any other way. But how can we face this reality with a proper Christian perspective? Let's look at Nehemiah's personal example in this area.

1. *We should accept promotions as a blessing from God.* There are some Christians who are afraid of advancement, particularly positions involving significant responsibility and authority. There seem to be several

reasons for this. First, we may fear failure. That is natural for most of us. Second, we may not want to accept the accountability that must always go with responsibility. And third, we may feel advancement is somehow wrong and inappropriate for Christians, that we are in some respects to be "seen and not heard."

Obviously, there is no question but that we must think carefully before we accept increased responsibility. Increased income and benefits may not in the long haul compensate for the demands that are placed upon us and the price we have to pay in terms of time and effort. It is not wrong to count the cost, particularly when it affects our biblical priorities. For example, it is never right to sacrifice our family on the altar of promotion. That is too great a price to pay.

But on the other hand, as Christians, our motivation for advancement must be based upon more than personal cost to us. And it must also be based upon more than an increased salary and other benefits. We must view the opportunity in terms of what God can do through us.

One reason for accepting increased responsibility is that it always provides opportunities for personal growth. It stretches us, giving us opportunities to increase our faith, to intensify our prayer lives, to develop our potential, to learn new skills, to improve our relationships with people and to raise our tolerance level for handling difficult situations.

New demands usually bring periods of emotional pain, but without these experiences we tend to maintain the status quo. We actually need a certain amount of stress to grow spiritually and psychologically. This was why James wrote: "Consider it all joy, my brethren, when you encounter various trials; knowing that the testing of your faith produces endurance. And let endurance have its perfect result, that you may be perfect and complete, lacking in nothing" (Jas. 1:2-4).

A second reason that we should consider accepting promotions and advancement is because it does improve our financial situation. It enables us to be more comfortable and free from worry and concern and increases our security in life, which in turn can enable us to be far more productive. Our energies, rather than being dissipated through worry, can be channeled into practical projects that will honor and glorify God.

But even more important, increased income enables us to give more, to meet others' needs and to advance the work of the church. For those who have learned the joy of giving, it not only provides personal blessing, but untold blessings for those who are recipients of their graciousness. And God has told us we are to give proportionately as we prosper (see 1 Cor. 16:2).

There's a third reason we should consider advancement. It is perhaps more important than any of the above. *Increased responsibility and authority enables us as Christians to have a stronger platform for Christian witness* and to create working conditions that will benefit and help others. In our culture, we need many more Christians directing the affairs of life. This is why we read in Proverbs: "When the righteous increase, the people rejoice, but when a wicked man rules, people groan" (Prov. 29:2). May God give us more righteous leaders at all levels in our society—in the business world, in educational institutions, in the political arena, and perhaps most important of all, in the church.

2. Promotion could bring temptation. Though we should view promotions as a blessing from God, we must also realize that it opens the door to new temptations. This is particularly true of course if the position brings with it unusual privileges, such as it did when Nehemiah was appointed governor of Jerusalem. Because this was the highest position in Israel, it opened the door of temptation to many governors before Nehemiah, who, seemingly without giving it a second thought, walked through the door and abused their privileges.

It is a fact of life that few people handle advancement well. Thomas Carlyle, a Scottish historian, once wrote, "Adversity is hard on a man; but for one man who can stand prosperity, there are a hundred that will stand adversity."[1]

Charles Swindoll, keying on the same idea, states: "Few people can live in the lap of luxury and maintain their spiritual, emotional, and moral equilibrium. Sudden elevation often disturbs balance, which leads to pride and a sense of self-sufficiency—and then, a fall. It's ironic, but more of us can hang tough through a demotion than through a promotion. And it is at this level a godly leader shows himself or herself strong. The right kind of leaders, when promoted, know how to handle the honor."[2]

Though statistics do indicate that few people can handle significant advancement and promotion without losing their psychological and spiritual bearings, Nehemiah illustrates with his life that it *can* be done and demonstrates for us *how* it can be done. And foundational to his success in handling his position of power and prestige was the fact that he was committed to certain goals.

First, he was determined to never abuse his privileges. And we must have the same goals. Practically speaking, this means we must never use our position as a platform to pad our pockets, to exploit others, or become guilty of a conflict of interest. Every individual who is promoted to a position in top management in our own culture faces these temptations regularly. With management advancement comes trust and new freedom. And if we are not committed to certain values, we can misuse expense accounts, exploit people to further our own personal interests and use company time to build our own personal empire.

Nehemiah faced these very temptations. The opportunity was there. Other governors before him had done it all. And the people probably even expected it to happen again. They were resigned to it. But Nehemiah did not succumb to this kind of temptation. He refused to fall prey to selfish ambition. What a lesson this is to twentieth-century Christians who are promoted to significant positions of leadership in our own society.

A second reason Nehemiah did not lose his psychological and spiritual equilibrium as a leader in Israel is that he actually refused to use some of the privileges he was entitled to, primarily because of the economic conditions that existed when he took over as governor. The facts are, he could have insisted on his food allowance, and no one would have questioned his behavior. But because the people were under great stress financially at this time in their history, because he was asking them to personally sacrifice in rebuilding the wall, and because he had sufficient personal resources to care for the food allowance himself—he did not insist on using his privileges.

There may be times in our own society, especially in the Christian community when privileges should be refused. Paul illustrates this dramatically in his own ministry. He often gave up his own rights as an apostle so as to help people understand more clearly the true nature of the gospel, that it is a free gift from God. Writing to the Corinthians he said, "Am I not free? Am I not an apostle. . .? Do we not have a right to eat and drink. . .? Who at any time serves as a soldier at his own expense? Who plants a vineyard, and does not eat the fruit of it? Or who tends a flock and does not use the milk of the flock. . .? If we sowed spiritual things in you, is it too much if we should reap material things from you? If others share the right over you, do we not more? Nevertheless, *we did not use this right,* but we endure all things, that we may cause no hindrance to the gospel of Christ" (1 Cor. 9:1,4,7,11,12).

In many ways Nehemiah was an Old Testament Apostle Paul. He knew there were times when it was best to give up his own rights in order to achieve God's purposes on earth. Though this is not a normal expectation from leadership, there are times when it is the best thing to do. It is a true test of our motives. And this leads to our final point.

3. We must approach promotion with proper motives. There were three factors that motivated Nehemiah in his decision-making process as governor of Jerusalem. He feared God, he was sensitive to people's needs and he desired God's special blessing in his life. If we as Christians approach advancement and promotion with these same basic motivations, we have the key to maintaining our psychological and spiritual equilibrium. Let's look at them one by one.

Nehemiah feared God. He made it very clear that his ethical behavior as governor was motivated by his personal relationship with God. Speaking of the exploitation engaged in by previous governors, he stated unequivocally, "I did not do so because of the fear of God" (5:15).

As stated in our previous chapter, part of Nehemiah's appeal to the rich in Israel who were taking advantage of the poor was what God had stated in the Law. They were in direct violation of His will, and the Lord had made it very clear that His day-to-day blessing upon Israel was dependent upon their obedience. Nehemiah, of course, applied these truths to his own life. His fear of God related to the fact that he did not want to be guilty of violating God's law, and having to suffer the consequences.

Today many Christians ignore this principle. One reason is that we take God's promise of blessings upon the righteous and unrighteous for granted (see Matt. 5:45). Furthermore, we have often used "fear" inappropriately, giving Christians the impression that God is ready to pounce on them and punish them the moment they disobey

Him. Teaching regarding the "fear of God" has not been balanced with the "love of God."

But on the other hand we have often gone from one extreme to the other and often, in our behavior, ignored God's Word. Because He does not reach down out of heaven and deal with us directly, we take His grace for granted.

As Christians we must realize that if we disobey God we *will* ultimately pay the consequences. Frequently, we dig our own grave over a period of time. Putting it yet another way, we often little by little undermine ourselves until some day we will reap the natural consequences, even in this life. Furthermore, we will reap even more serious consequences when we stand before God, ashamed because of our failure to live our lives in the light of His greatness and His authority over us.

Today we need more godly fear. Rightly defined, this means that we stand in awe of who God is and what He has done for us, and that eventually we will have to give an account to Him for how we have lived our lives on earth.

The New Testament adds another significant dimension to this motivational factor. Not only should we live godly lives because of godly fear, but because of His grace and love toward us. Thus Paul wrote to Titus: "For the *grace of God* has appeared, bringing salvation to all men, instructing us to deny ungodliness and worldy desires and to live sensibly, righteously and godly in the present age" (Titus 2:11,12). In fact, since we can live our lives in the full light of what God has done for us in Jesus Christ, this fact should motivate us even more strongly than the fear of God. We now know what it cost the Father to redeem us from His forthcoming judgment on all of those who do not accept His grace and love.

A second motivational factor in Nehemiah's life-style as governor was a sensitivity to people. He would not allow himself to even receive what he was entitled to when he knew it would only increase the burden on the poor in Israel. Using his own words, he said, "I did not demand the governor's food allowance, *because the servitude was heavy on this people*" (5:18).

Christians who are sensitive to others will not take advantage of them. They will not use their positions of power to exploit people. Rather, they will use this opportunity to help people, to make their lives more comfortable and to create better living and working conditions. A dedicated Christian's goal will be that of Christ—to become a greater servant as his position of authority and power increases. When Christians are motivated by this kind of thinking, they can handle almost any promotion without falling prey to Satan's tactics.

Nehemiah desired to be favored by God. Nehemiah made it abundantly clear, not only in this passage before us but in other places in his historical account, that part of his motivation toward right behavior related to his desire to please God and consequently to be rewarded by God. Thus, he ended the passage, "Remember me, O my God, for good, according to all that I have done for this people" (5:19).

It is not wrong to do good in order to be favored by God. He has promised that He will reward us. In the New Testament, the greatest emphasis is on eternal rewards, but it does not exclude earthly rewards. Though it should always be a secondary motivation, as it was in Nehemiah's life, it is natural to expect blessing from God when we obey Him.

Joshua certainly illustrates this in his own role as leader of Israel. To him God said, "This book of the law shall not depart from your mouth, but you shall meditate on it day and night, so that you may be careful to do according to all that is written in it; for *then* you will make your way prosperous, and then you will have success" (Josh. 1:8).

And Paul underscores this basic motivation when he wrote to the Philippians and thanked them for their sacrificial gift to him while he was in prison. "And my God," Paul wrote to them reassuringly, "shall supply all *your* needs according to His riches in glory in Christ Jesus" (Phil. 4:19). In other words, Paul was confident that God would reward them—even in this life—because they had shared their material possessions with him.

Life Response

How are you handling the promotional opportunities God is bringing into your life? Furthermore, what is your attitude toward those opportunities that will ordinarily come in the future? Following is a prayer of commitment that will help you both now and when opportunities come your way.

Dear God,

I will accept with gratitude the opportunities for advancement you allow to come my way. I will, however, count the cost to me personally, and particularly to my family so that I will not violate any biblical priorities. But I will not withdraw simply because I fear failure or am unwilling to accept the accountability that accompanies the responsibility. Nor will I refuse the opportunity because of the misguided point of view that Christians should not seek or consider prestigious positions.

On the other hand, I realize that Satan will work harder in my life if I accept advancement. To counter these attacks I will use the position as an opportunity to grow spiritually. I will consider this promotion as a better platform to also advance my Christian witness. Though I believe it is appropriate to use my improved financial situation to create a greater sense of security for my family, I will also do all I can to be a good steward and give more to advance the work of your church. I will never abuse the privileges accompanying my promotion, financially or in any other way. I will not exploit others or become guilty of a conflict of interest.

To accomplish these goals I will discharge my responsibilities in the fear of God, realizing He alone has made this opportunity possible. I will also do all I can to use my position as a servant to others, meeting their needs and improving their lot in life. In turn, Lord, I believe you will reward me personally now and eternally because I view my work as your work and because I have been faithful to your principles. I will do all I can to make sure my motives honor you first and foremost and not myself.

> In Jesus' name, Amen.
> Signed _____

Notes
1. John Bartlett, *Familiar Quotations* (Boston: Little, Brown and Company, 1955), p. 475.
2. Charles Swindoll, *Hand Me Another Brick* (Nashville: Thomas Nelson, Inc., 1978), p. 113.

10

Nehemiah's
Most Difficult Test

Nehemiah 6:1-14

Under Nehemiah's leadership the wall surrounding Jerusalem was rebuilt in an incredible 52 days. Even the enemies of Israel recognized this accomplishment as a miracle engineered not only by Nehemiah and the children of Israel but by God Himself (see Neh. 6:16).

However, during this brief but action-packed two-month period, Israel—and Nehemiah particularly—faced some very difficult problems. Not only did they have to sacrifice time, energy and personal resources but they encountered intense opposition from their enemies who again and again tried to stop the building process.

The majority of these attacks were precipitated by Sanballat the Horonite, Tobiah the Ammonite, and Geshem the Arab. When these men first heard that Nehemiah had come from Susa to Jerusalem to "seek the welfare of the sons of Israel," they were very unhappy and displeased (2:10). And when they saw the children of Israel actually "put their hands to the good work" (2:18), their displeasure was translated into action. They "mocked . . . and despised" God's people (see 2:19).

But Israel was not to be denied. The more they were threatened and verbally attacked, the harder they worked. Sanballat particularly was highly threatened by all of this activity. His negative emotions intensified! He "became furious and very angry" (4:1). And while on a more direct course of action, they received word that the "wall was joined together to half its height" (4:6).

When Sanballat, Tobiah and Geshem heard this report they knew they had to do more than talk. Consequently, they "conspired together" to secretly attack Jerusalem from all sides (see 4:7,8). But their plan was discovered and Israel prepared themselves for the attack. Consequently, it never happened and the work went on until the wall was completed. All that needed to be done was to "set up the doors in the gates" (6:1). And once again we meet Sanballat, Tobiah and Geshem, making one final effort to stop the work. And this effort was the most subtle of all, and their sole object was Nehemiah. At this juncture they knew it was their only chance. If they could only remove him from the scene, or at least destroy his credibility in Israel, they might be able to yet achieve their goal. This is what chapter 6 in the book of Nehemiah is all about. Nehemiah himself describes three subtle attacks on him personally. Each was different, but each was designed to destory Nehemiah—if not his life, at least his effectiveness as a leader in Israel.

The First Scheme (Neh. 6:1-4)

The first attack was the most subtle. Sanballat and Geshem invited Nehemiah to meet with them "at Chephirim in the plain of Ono" (6:2).[1] On the surface it appeared that they wanted to have a peace conference with Nehemiah, but their hidden motive was to harm Nehemiah (v. 2) perhaps even kill him. To the casual observer, it seemed they were saying, "Alright Nehemiah! You win! Let's get together and talk about it. There is no need continuing a cold war. In fact, you pick the place in Ono, and we'll meet you there."

Nehemiah of course was more than a casual observer. He suspected foul play and he was right! But, at that moment he had no way to prove it. To question their motives outright would only intensify their anger and would make him look bad, particularly to those in Israel who were sympathetic to Tobiah (see 6:17-19). And of course he always had to face the possibility that they *were* sincere.

Though Nehemiah could not prove his enemies' motives at that moment, he chose a method that would eventually demonstrate whether or not they were sincere. He simply "sent messengers to them, saying, 'I'm doing a great work and I cannot come down. Why should the work stop while I leave it and come down to you?'" (6:3).

By responding in this way, Nehemiah was *not* openly questioning their motives. His answer was logical and reasonable. Sincere people would understand his response. In fact, he gave Sanballat and Geshem an opportunity to prove that their motives were sincere, that they really wanted to make peace. After all, it would be just as easy if not easier for them to come to him.

Sanballat and Geshem's response tipped their hand. Rather than countering with an offer to meet with Nehemiah in Jerusalem, they sent the same message four times, and Nehemiah responded four times—in the very same way. Four times he gave them an opportunity to prove the sincerity of their motives.

How easy it would have been for Nehemiah, upon the third or fourth request, to attack their motives, to accuse them of insincerity in an attempt to harm him. But he patiently waited it out until *they* revealed their motives. And this they did, with their fifth response.

The Second Scheme (Neh. 6:5-9)

When it became obvious to Nehemiah's enemies that he would not leave Jerusalem and meet with them at a so-called peace conference, they tried another tactic.

A Pressure Tactic

They put pressure on him, trying to force him to meet with them in the plain of Ono. Sanballat's servant arrived on the scene a fifth time, but on this occasion he read an open letter to Nehemiah, which is as follows: "It is reported among the nations, and Gashmu [Geshem] says, that you and the Jews are planning to rebel; therefore you are rebuilding the wall. And you are to be their king, according to these reports. And you have also appointed prophets to proclaim in Jerusalem concerning you, 'A king is in Judah!' And now it will be reported to the king according to these reports. So come now, let us take counsel together" (6:6,7). As you analyze this letter carefully, there are several subtle and insidious aspects.

First, it appears on the surface that they have Nehemiah's welfare at heart. They seem to convey the idea that they know these reports are just rumors, but by the same token, they make it clear that if King Artaxerxes hears about it, he won't know they're rumors. Consequently, they attempted to give Nehemiah the impression that they wanted to get together to discuss the matter in order to protect Nehemiah. Though they worded the letter to give this impression, obviously this was not their intent.

Second, and more basic to their motive, they were attempting to get Nehemiah to respond out of fear. They knew that King Artaxerxes trusted him to be a loyal subject when he authorized him to come to Jerusalem.

Nehemiah's natural reaction would be to protect himself against this possible misunderstanding.

Third, Nehemiah's enemies were probably using an element of truth. This is the most subtle tactic of all. It is quite probable that some well-meaning religious leaders in Judah had interpreted Nehemiah's presence and accomplishments in Jerusalem as a fulfillment of some of the Old Testament prophecies regarding the coming king and messiah. For example, some patriotic preacher may have spoken on Zechariah 9:9, "Behold, your king is coming to you; He is just and endowed with salvation." It is easy to see how someone may have applied this statement about Jesus Christ to Nehemiah.

Fourth, by reading this letter publicly, Nehemiah's enemies were putting public pressure on Nehemiah to respond. The casual hearer could easily interpret this letter as suggesting a good course of action to protect not only Nehemiah but all of Israel. After all, if these reports *did* get back to King Artaxerxes, he could very quickly issue a decree—as he had done before—to stop the work. This time, however, he might take more serious action against the Jews. There is no doubt it could at least mean death for Nehemiah.

Nehemiah's Bold Response

Knowing all this, Nehemiah's response was straight-forward and very bold and demonstrated unusual trust in God.

First, he denied the accusations. He and the Jews were *not* "planning to rebel." This was *not* why they were "rebuilding the wall." He was *not* planning to "be their king." He had *not* appointed prophets to proclaim a king is in Judah (6:6,7). These were not true statements and he told them so: "Such things as you are saying have not been done, but you are inventing them in your own mind" (6:8). At this juncture Nehemiah was not being defensive;

rather, he was honestly and openly defending the truth.

*The second thing Nehemiah did as a result of the open
letter was to interpret the situation to himself* and perhaps
to others who had heard the letter read. Our enemies are
"trying to frighten us," he said. They want us to "become
discouraged with the work and it will not be done" (6:9).

And finally, he prayed. Nehemiah did again what he
had done so often before in crisis situations. He lifted his
heart to God and prayed: "But now, O God, strengthen my
hands" (6:9). The content of this prayer seems to indicate
that this was a difficult time for Nehemiah. He needed
divine strength and help. And, humanly speaking, it's
understandable. No human being, no matter how capable,
enjoys being openly accused falsely. No person delights in
having his motives misinterpreted. No one feels comfortable when his "good is evil spoken of" (see Rom. 14:6).
And no person enjoys being accused of being on an ego
trip when the facts are that he has sacrificed greatly to help
others achieve their own goals. All of these accusations
had been hurled at Nehemiah by means of this open letter,
when in reality he was above reproach. If there was any
doubt before, Nehemiah now knew for sure that they were
planning to harm him. And once again he refused to
cooperate, in spite of the fear the letter generated.

The Third Scheme (Neh. 6:10-14)

Nehemiah's enemies persisted in their evil planning.
Their next plot was to try to destroy his credibility in
Israel. Consequently, they hired a man on the inside to
propose a solution to Nehemiah. His name was Shemaiah.
We know nothing of him, except that he claimed to be a
prophet. It appears that part of his strategy was to purpose-
ly lock himself in his house and to send word for Nehemiah to come visit him. He evidently structured an urgent
situation that would arouse Nehemiah's curiosity.

Shemaiah must have been a man Nehemiah had confidence in, for it would be illogical for him to visit someone secretively whom he did not trust. When Nehemiah arrived, Shemaiah's message was direct and to the point: "Let us meet together in the house of God, within the temple, and let us close the doors of the temple, for they are coming to kill you, and they are coming to kill you at night" (6:10). There were two fatal flaws in Shemaiah's so-called prophecy.

First, it would not be logical for God to ask Nehemiah to flee at this juncture. The Lord had miraculously made it possible for Nehemiah to come to Jerusalem, and had protected him from his enemies again and again during the building process. After all, the project was in actuality completed, except they had not set up the doors and the gates. It would not make sense for Nehemiah to flee at this moment. Furthermore, it would have destroyed the confidence Israel had in him as a leader. They would not understand such actions from the one who had been their encourager. Consequently, Nehemiah exclaimed, "Should a man like me flee?" Putting it more graphically, "Should the one who had been appointed by God to lead Israel to rebuild this wall suddenly turn and run?"

The second flaw in Shemaiah's "prophetic message" was to report that God had asked Nehemiah to violate His law. Nehemiah was not a priest. And as a layman, to enter and shut himself in the temple—literally within the holy place—would be to desecrate the house of God and to bring himself under God's judgment (see Num. 18:7).

Putting these two observations together convinced Nehemiah that Shemaiah was a false prophet, employed by his enemies to trick him (see Neh. 6:12). And, as Nehemiah reported in his narrative, he saw clearly why it all happened: "He was hired for this reason, that I might become frightened and act accordingly and sin, so that they might have an evil report in order that they could reproach me" (6:13).

One way or another, Nehemiah's enemies were determined to stop what was happening in Jerusalem. They were willing to stoop to any means to achieve their goals. Perhaps the most subtle aspect of the final scheme was to capitalize on the fears they had already generated in Nehemiah's heart by trying to convince him that the God who had called him to Jerusalem in the first place, was now telling him through Shemaiah the prophet to run for his life. And to make matters even more difficult, Shemaiah was evidently only one of several who tried to deceive him. Thus, Nehemiah concludes this episode by praying, "Remember, O my God, Tobiah and Sanballat according to these works of theirs, and also Noadiah the prophetess and the *rest of the prophets* who were trying to frighten me" (6:14).

Responding to Human Conflict Today

Most of us as Christians cannot identify directly with Nehemiah's frustrating encounters with Sanballat, Tobiah and Geshem. There are few Christians living in our culture who face threats on their lives. In fact, few of us have enemies who deliberately and maliciously attempt to destroy our reputation and credibility, although there are instances when this happens.

However, *how* Nehemiah responded to the difficulties he faced in Jerusalem exemplifies for us how we can respond to all levels of human conflict, whether they involve a deceptive and malicious attack on one end of the social continuum, or naive and sincere criticism on the opposite end. What are these lessons?

1. We must be wise in the way we respond. This is perhaps the greatest lesson we can learn from Nehemiah. And this wisdom can be outlined as follows:
● Don't counterattack by questioning the other person's motives. Perhaps the person's motives are wrong, but in

most instances we have no way to really know. Even Nehemiah, who had every reason to question his enemies' motives on the basis of their past behavior, did not challenge their motives in his response. Rather, he refused to meet with them on the basis of what was an honest priority responsibility. "I am doing a great work," he responded, "and I cannot come down" (6:3). Though this did not satisfy Sanballat and the others, it did not openly give them further opportunity to try to prove to their friends in Israel that Nehemiah, not they, was the uncooperative culprit.

And remember, what appears to be a dishonest motive may actually be sincere. Though it was highly improbable that Nehemiah's enemies had undergone a change of heart, he had to allow for that possibility, especially since he had no way of knowing what was actually going on in their hearts. People *do* change!

I'm reminded of a situation where a husband was very insensitive to his wife and children for many years. And for years this woman tolerated his behavior, hoping for change. Eventually, she couldn't emotionally handle the problem any more. She left her husband and filed for a divorce. Then, the man began to change. He didn't want to lose his wife or family. From all outward appearances he was making unusual effort to become a different person— psychologically and spiritually. However, everything he did was interpreted by his estranged wife as being based on a false motive. In her mind, he couldn't be sincere. In her eyes, and on the basis of past behavior, he *had* to be engaging in manipulative behavior.

It is easy to understand this woman's fear. But it is also true that people do change. And if they haven't, if their motives *are* wrong, they'll eventually reveal them. And that's what happened in Nehemiah's situation, which is our next lesson in wisdom from Nehemiah's response.

● Be patient and wait for motives to be revealed through

overt behavior. Nehemiah's enemies eventually revealed their true motives. Four times they suggested a peace conference designed to harm him. Four times he responded in the same way, "I can't come down now." And the fifth time, they tipped their hand. They changed their strategy which gave Nehemiah an opportunity to respond to concrete facts.

As Christians, we must be patient in the area of human conflict. Malicious motives will eventually come to the surface. And if people are critical because they don't understand our motives, they will eventually have a change of heart if we continue to be open, sincere, and nondefensive. And remember too, sincere people sometimes misinterpret our motives wrongly because we aren't being very *wise* in our own approach to solving problems. It is a good rule of thumb to keep in mind that most Christians are not out to hurt or harm other Christians. In fact, most non-Christians in our culture do not have that motive. Criticism is usually based on misunderstandings or unwise actions and responses on our part. We must not allow ourselves to become paranoid. If we believe everyone is out to get us, we have a serious personal problem.

● A third point of wisdom in handling criticism, particularly from non-Christians, is outlined for us in the New Testament. The apostle Peter dealt with this problem in his first Epistle. Writing to Christians scattered throughout various sections of the New Testament world who were being persecuted by non-Christians, he gave them some very wise instruction. His words speak for themselves:

"Keep your behavior excellent among the Gentiles, so that in the thing in which they *slander* you as evildoers, they may on account of your *good deeds,* as they observe them, glorify God in the day of visitation" (1 Pet. 2:12).

"For such is the will of God that by *doing right* you may *silence* the ignorance of foolish men" (1 Pet. 2:15).

"But sanctify Christ as Lord in your hearts, always

being ready to make a *defense* to every one who asks you to give an account for the hope that is in you, yet with *gentleness* and *reverence;* and keep a good conscience so that in the thing in which you are *slandered,* those who revile your good behavior in Christ may be put to shame" (1 Pet. 3:15,16).

2. *We must be bold in our response to rumors but never attempt to take revenge.* Nehemiah's enemies revealed their true motives to actually harm him by starting a rumor which they hoped would force him to meet with them. Nehemiah's response outlines for us a very biblical way to handle this kind of public pressure.

• Deny the false accusations to those who started them with a straightforward but sensitive and nondefensive response. This is what Nehemiah did when it was rumored by his enemies that he was trying to set himself up as king in Israel (see Neh. 6:8). And in the New Testament, Paul the apostle probably illustrates this approach more clearly than any other Christian. He was constantly being attacked by both non-Christians and Christians: non-Christians often threatened his life (see 2 Cor. 11:24-26); Christians often questioned his motives. But his response was always straightforward, sensitive and nondefensive. It is one thing to present a defense; it's another to be defensive.

• Like Nehemiah, interpret the situation to those closest to you who really know the truth. People who know us well, who are our real friends, are our greatest defenders. We must let them speak for us, particularly to those who have been influenced by false rumors.

• Like Nehemiah, pray for personal strength to endure the anxiety and stress caused by false rumors. It was not easy emotionally or physically for Nehemiah to face the accusations brought against him by his enemies. Thus he prayed, "But now, O God, strengthen my hands" (6:9). Nor is it easy for any one of us to be falsely accused, to have our motives questioned. But God can strengthen us in times like these and actually enrich our lives. There are lessons we can learn—including the possibility that we may have actually opened the door to rumors through unwise behavior. Though this was not true in Nehemiah's case, it certainly can be true with any one of us in our relationships with others.

● There is another lesson that comes from the New Testament. We should also pray for those who hurt us—whether maliciously or naively. Charles Colson, who was imprisoned because of his involvement in Watergate, perhaps illustrates these steps in handling false accusations in the modern-day world more clearly than any other Christian. Following his release from prison, he was seriously implicated in a newspaper article which accused him—at least by innuendo—of being part of a murder plot against a newspaper columnist. His response initially was one of great anger. He relates his reactions in his book, *Life Sentence,* an exciting sequel to *Born Again:*

> The article referred to a senior official who, it was reported, had ordered Hunt to do Anderson in. That narrowed it to a few of us. Then came this sentence: "Charles Colson, the former White House special counsel who recruited Hunt for White House work, said yesterday that he had never heard of the plan." I slammed the paper on the kitchen table. That was the same as naming me; readers would draw only one inference.
>
> Patty [Colson's wife] couldn't cheer me up. "What do you mean 'smile'?" I growled at her. "I've been accused of a lot of wild things but not murder!"

Eventually, Colson met with his close Christi

brothers at Fellowship House to seek counsel as to what to do. Together they considered one basic question: "How does a Christian handle false accusations?"

> My inclination was to battle back, protest, proclaim my innocence.
>
> The others shook their heads. "Anything you say, Chuck, will be twisted," noted Harold. "Let's find out how Jesus handled these situations. He was falsely accused more times than any man in history."
>
> The minute Harold spoke, I knew the answer. I had been reading the Beatitudes only a week before. Jesus had told His disciples: "Blessed are you when men revile you and persecute you and utter all kinds of evil against you falsely on my account. Rejoice and be glad, for your reward is great in heaven" (Matthew 5:11-12, *RSV*).
>
> Did this statement apply to me? Was I being falsely accused because of my stand for Christ? Far from it. Still, as a Christian, shouldn't my response to unfair accusation be the same? I was to accept the attack without defending myself. While I wasn't quite able to "rejoice and be glad" in the situation, I did turn it over to the Lord. But it was tough to do, I discovered.

As weeks passed the story faded out of the news. However, Colson's greatest concern was that the false accusation still remained in the minds of millions of people. "It is a terrifying experience," he wrote, "to be associated with a 'murder plot,' yet I see it now that this episode was used to prepare me for even more difficult testings."[2]

Charles Colson's response was not an easy one, nor did it suddenly remove the emotional pain or the problem. But eventually he was understood by the populace through his Christian life-style and through the witness of those who really knew him and defended him. It was a direct fulfillment of Peter's words to the Christians in the New Testament world. Many people have glorified God because they've observed a Christian's "good deeds" (1 Pet. 2:12). In "doing right" we put to "silence the ignorance of foolish men" (1 Pet. 2:15). And eventually most of those who revile "good behavior in Christ" are put to shame (1 Pet. 3:16).

What worked for Nehemiah in the Old Testament, for Paul in the New Testament, for Chuck Colson in the twentieth-century arena, will also work for any one of us. They denied the accusation to those who made it. They interpreted the situation to those closest to them who knew the truth, and they prayed! They then left the rest up to God.

Let us always remember the words of Paul: "Never take your own revenge, beloved, but leave room for the wrath of God, for it is written, 'Vengeance is Mine, I will repay, says the Lord" (Rom. 12:19). God's will is that we "not be overcome by evil," but rather that we "overcome evil with good" (Rom. 12:21).

3. We must not allow fear to cloud our perceptions in thinking and cause us to act impulsively and do something foolish. This motive was foundational in most of what Nehemiah's enemies had done, particularly when he did not respond to their initial invitation. They wanted to *frighten* him with the thought that Artaxerxes would get wind of the "fact" that he was trying to set up his own kingdom in Judah. They also tried to discourage him, to cause him to leave the work and flee, perhaps to return to

Susa to prove to the king that these rumors were false. They tried to frighten him with a false prophecy from God regarding proposed threats on his life. But in the midst of all of this, Nehemiah did not allow his very real fear to cause him to act irrationally.

There is a great lesson for all of us in Nehemiah's example. How easy it is to try to defend ourselves; to counterattack; to spend all of our time and energy protecting our image and being sidetracked from our primary work and responsibility. Yes, there are things we *must* do, as just illustrated from Nehemiah's approach to the problem. But beyond that we must follow Jesus' example, which is so clearly stated in the epistle to the Hebrews: "Therefore, since we have so great a cloud of witnesses surrounding us, let us also lay aside every encumbrance, and the sin which so easily entangles us, and let us run with endurance the race that is set before us, fixing our eyes on Jesus the author and perfecter of faith, who for the joy set before Him endured the cross, despising the shame, and has sat down at the right hand of the throne of God. For consider Him who has endured such hostility by sinners against Himself, so that you may not grow weary and lose heart" (Heb. 12:1-3).

Life Response
When you are criticized, either maliciously or sincerely, how do you respond? Rate yourself on the following evaluation scales in order to determine your areas of strength as well as your areas of need:

1. I am wise in the way I respond.

☐ I do not counterattack or question others' motives.

Unsatisfactory   *1   2   3   4   5*   *Satisfactory*

☐ I am patient and wait for motives to be revealed as right or wrong through specific actions that cannot be misinterpreted.

Unsatisfactory   *1   2   3   4   5*   *Satisfactory*

☐ If falsely accused, I continue to live a consistent Christian life, knowing that eventually I will be vindicated in the eyes of those who are seeking truth.

Unsatisfactory   *1   2   3   4   5*   *Satisfactory*

☐ I try to learn from these experiences, realizing that I may be bringing some of this on myself because of my own *unwise* behavior.

Unsatisfactory   *1   2   3   4   5*   *Satisfactory*

2. I am *bold* in responding to rumors, but I do not take revenge.

☐ In a straightforward, sensitive and nondefensive way, I deny the rumors to those who have stated them.

Unsatisfactory   *1   2   3   4   5*   *Satisfactory*

☐ I interpret the situation to those who are close to me and also who really know the truth and who will be able to defend me to those who have been negatively influenced by the rumor.

Unsatisfactory   *1   2   3   4   5*   *Satisfactory*

☐ I pray for personal strength emotionally and physically to handle the anxiety and stress that is caused by this experience.

Unsatisfactory   *1   2   3   4   5*   *Satisfactory*

☐ I pray for those who have hurt me, whether maliciously or naively.

Unsatisfactory   *1   2   3   4   5*   *Satisfactory*

3. I do not allow fear to cloud my thinking so as to act irrationally and do something foolish.

Unsatisfactory   *1   2   3   4   5*   *Satisfactory*

Notes

1. We're not sure of the exact location of the meeting place suggested by Sanballat and Geshem. C.F. Keil believes it was probably northwest of Jerusalem, not far from Bethel.

2. Charles W. Colson, *Life Sentence* (Lincoln, VA: Chosen Books, 1979). pp. 51,52.

11

Nehemiah's
Faithful Co-Worker

Nehemiah 8:1—9:38

Once Nehemiah had led the children of Israel in successfully completing the wall, several things happened. First, he assigned two faithful men—his brother, Hanani, and another man named Hanaiah—to take charge of the military and security operations in Jerusalem (see 7:1-3). He then conducted a careful census to discover who had actually returned from exile (see 7:4-73). Under the pressure of rebuilding the wall, it had been impossible to make a complete record of everyone who lived in Judah.

At this juncture, Ezra, a priest and scribe once again entered the scene. He was no stranger in Israel. He had returned to Jerusalem approximately 14 years before Nehemiah, also with the blessing of King Artaxerxes (see Ezra 7:11-28). His primary purpose was to teach the children of Israel the law of God.

Nehemiah would be the first to acknowledge that to a great extent his own success in Jerusalem was due to Ezra's diligent and faithful ministry among the people of Israel. Ezra was a man who was deeply committed to understanding and obeying God's will. And more than that, he was committed to teaching others the will of God. This is clear from the book that bears his name, for we read, "Ezra had set his heart to *study* the law of the Lord, and to *practice* it, and to *teach* His statutes and ordinances in Israel" (Ezra 7:10).

This statement about Ezra communicates volumes regarding this man's relationship with God. Though his calling in life specified that he was one of those who was especially responsible to teach the laws of God to the children of Israel, he made sure he did his personal homework before he tried to communicate with others.

First, he carefully *studied* the Scriptures. He knew that before he could teach God's truth effectively to others, he had to understand it himself.

Second, he not only studied God's laws, but he made sure he applied their truth to his own life before he tried to get others to respond in obedience. He had "set his heart . . . to *practice* it." He did not ask people to do something he himself was not doing. This also explains why we read of Ezra, "The hand of the Lord His God was upon him" (Ezra 7:6,9). Because Ezra was personally committed to both *knowing* and *doing* the will of God, the Lord granted him favor among those in the pagan environment as well as those in Israel.

Ezra's Arrival in Jerusalem

When Ezra first arrived in Jerusalem, the moral and spiritual condition of the people was deplorable. But as he prayerfully began his teaching ministry among the people, gradually they began to respond in obedience to the laws of God. And it was in the midst of this process that

Nehemiah arrived in Jerusalem and challenged them to trust God to help them rebuild the walls.

This larger perspective helps clarify Nehemiah's success. Without Ezra's years of preparation, the people would not have been ready to accept such a challenge. It is in this larger context that they said, "Let us arise and build," and then "put their hands to the good work" (Neh. 2:18).

Ezra's preliminary work is also reflected in the behavior of the people once the walls were completed. The two-month building process was an interlude in the educational experience, but it was also a means to motivate the people to want to know more of God's law. They themselves asked Ezra to continue his teaching ministry among them. We read that "all the people gathered as one man at the square which was in front of the Water Gate, and they asked Ezra the scribe to bring the book of the law of Moses which the Lord had given to Israel" (Neh. 8:1).

You can imagine how much this request must have thrilled Ezra. For years he had been trying to get them to listen. There had been times, particularly when he first arrived in Jerusalem, that he was so appalled at the immoral condition of the people that he had torn his garments and had pulled out some of the hair from his head and beard (see Ezra 9:3). Falling on his knees and with outstretched hands lifted to God, he had confessed the sins of the people. "O my God, I am ashamed and embarrassed to lift up my face to Thee, my God, for our iniquities have risen above our heads, and our guilt has grown even to the heavens" (Ezra 9:6).

How many days and weeks and perhaps even months Ezra prayed and wept before God for Israel, we do not know. We *do* know that while he was "praying and making confession, weeping and prostrating himself before the house of God," a large group of people involving whole families gathered one day and joined him in his weeping and confession (see 10:1). This must have been the beginning point of revival and renewal in Israel.

Ezra's Ministry at the Water Gate

How different it must have been for Ezra that day at the Water Gate. For days he had watched the people attack the project of rebuilding the walls against impossible odds. He had watched their response to Nehemiah's challenges. He had seen them lift their hearts in prayer to God. How thrilled he must have been to see their motivation to trust God to help them accomplish what humanly speaking was an impossible task. But how much more thrilled he must have been when the people themselves—once the walls were rebuilt—gathered on their own in front of the Water Gate and asked him once again to read from the law of God. All of his previous pain and agony over these people must have faded away in view of this present moment of their eagerness and openness to know more of the will of God.

Though my main point of application in this chapter does not relate to Ezra's difficult experiences as a scribe and priest, I believe those of us who are involved in various ministries can learn a great lesson from this Old Testament leader. It is easy to get discouraged in the ministry. And one of the primary causes of this discouragement is the way some Christians respond to our efforts. When tempted to be discouraged, remember Ezra. Remember his weeks and months of prayer and weeping before God, confessing the sins of the people. Remember the slow response—that it took time to both teach and model obedience to the will of God. It took patience and perseverance. But remember also that eventually the people *did* respond. Their hearts too were broken before the Lord. And the day came, 14 years later, when they asked for Ezra to share the Word of God. Should we not ask ourselves in times of discouragement and lack of response the question: "How much have I prayed and persevered for the people I minister to? How long have I been faithful?"

Ezra Read from the Law of God

What a sight it must have been! Ezra stood on a platform above the people behind the wooden podium that had been made especially for this occasion (see Neh. 8:4). On his right stood six men and on his left stood seven more. As he opened the book of the law, the people stood up to express their reverence for God's Word (see 8:5).

Then Ezra prayed. No doubt lifting his hands toward heaven, we read that he "blessed the Lord the great God" (8:6). The specific content of his prayer at this moment is not included in the biblical record, but we are given enough information to conclude that he may have voiced a prayer of blessing to God similar to that outlined in the opening part of the prayer of the people which is recorded in chapter 9. They also began with blessing: "May Thy glorious name be blessed" (9:5). Perhaps the people themselves were responding with the very words Ezra used before he read from the book of the law. When the Levites asked the people to arise and bless the Lord their God forever and ever, notice their response: "O may Thy glorious name be blessed and exalted above all blessing and praise! Thou alone art the Lord. Thou hast made the heavens, the heaven of heavens with all their host, the earth and all that is on it, the seas and all that is in them. Thou dost give life to all of them and the heavenly host bows down before Thee" (Neh. 9:5,6).

The response of the people to Ezra's prayer must have been an ecstatic experience for this old priest and scribe. For years he had labored diligently to communicate God's truth to the people. And now as he looked out over this vast crowd of people, numbering in the thousands and gathered in the Water Gate square, he saw them lift their hands toward heaven and they shouted, "Amen, Amen!" And evidently without prompting, they next fell on their knees and bowed low with their faces to the ground as they "worshiped the Lord" (8:6).

The Levites Explained the Law of God

Nehemiah does not explain in detail exactly how Ezra and the Levites read and explained God's law to this large crowd that may have numbered somewhere between 30 and 50 thousand people (see 7:66,67). However, we can somewhat reconstruct how it may have happened. It seems that Ezra must have read sections of the law in the presence of *all* the people (see 8:3). Then at certain points, the Levites must have circulated out among the people and interpreted and explained what Ezra had read as the people gathered in small groups, perhaps divided down by households (see 8:7,8).

Interpretation and explanation were especially important in this setting. Ezra had been reading from the Hebrew Bible and many of the people were probably no longer fluent in Hebrew because of the influence of the Babylonian culture. This was particularly true of the younger generation. Intermarriage with various non-Jewish groups had accentuated the problem of communication (see Neh. 13:24). Consequently, Nehemiah records that Ezra and the Levites "read from the book, from the law of God, translating *to give the sense* so that they understood the reading" (8:8).

The People Obeyed the Law of God

The true test of "hearing" and "understanding" God's Word is in *obeying*. Not only did the children of Israel demonstrate their eagerness to revere and understand the Word of God, but they immediately responded with obedience. Their positive attitudes were translated into appropriate actions.

First, what they heard touched their emotions. They

were overcome with godly sorrow. As their personal and corporate life-styles were brought under the searchlight of Scripture, they immediately saw that they had fallen far short of God's standard for their lives. They literally wept before the Lord (see 8:9).

Second, Israel's sincere repentance eventually turned to joy (see 8:10-12). The more they learned from the law of God, the more they understood the Lord's displeasure with their sins and also understood His longsuffering and patience and willingness to forgive and restore when His children respond in obedience. Encouraged by Nehemiah and Ezra and the Levites not to "mourn or weep" (8:9) any longer, but rather to celebrate, we read that, "The people went away to eat, to drink, to send portions and to celebrate a great festival, *because they understood* the words which had been made known to them" (8:12).

Third, the leaders in Israel began to assume their God-ordained responsibilities for spiritual leadership. Following the corporate gathering to hear the law, a more select group "gathered to Ezra the scribe that they might gain insight into the words of the law" (8:13). This of course is a key to deepening and sustaining renewal and revival. It must begin and continue at the leadership level. Again, this voluntary response must have been very encouraging to Ezra.

The fourth response was to celebrate the Feast of Tabernacles (see 8:14-18). This response grew naturally out of the third. As the leaders in Israel learned more of God's will for their lives, they discovered that the Lord had designed a special experience for all of them that was to take place during the Feast of Tabernacles. For seven days they were to live in temporary shelters, which were called "booths" (see Lev. 23:33-44; Deut. 16:13-15). On the surface this may seem strange to the average twentieth-century Christian, but God's rationale for this experience was profound. For years the children of Israel had wandered in the wilderness living in temporary dwellings. On the one hand, this experience was prolonged because of Israel's unwillingness to obey God and enter the land. On the other hand, all during this time, God protected them and provided for their needs.

The picture is clear. God never wanted His people to forget this experience. More importantly, He did not want the younger generations in Israel to forget either His love for them or His judgment on them because of their sins (see Lev. 23:43).

Consequently, the leaders in Israel reinstated this special event. Whole families built booths and lived in them for seven days. You can imagine the questions that were asked by the children and youth in Israel, and the unique opportunity this afforded their parents to communicate their sacred history.

Their fifth response involved separation from pagan alliances and practices (Neh. 10:28-30). Separation of course did not mean *isolation,* for they could not remove themselves from their surroundings and environment. However, they determined to separate themselves from activities and involvements with unbelieving people that were in direct violation of the law of God—particularly intermarriage and idolatrous behavior.

Learning God's Word Today

What happened at the Water Gate so many years ago presents a biblical life-changing process for all of God's children. It illustrates how Christians today can maintain a proper relationship with Jesus Christ. Putting it succinctly, we too need to *read* the Scriptures, *understand* clearly what God says, and *apply* His truths specifically to our lives on a regular basis.

As twentieth-century Christians, particularly those of us who live in the English-speaking world, we are indeed fortunate. We have available not only the Old Testament, but God's complete written revelation. And in recent years modern translations have multiplied, making the Scriptures come alive with meaning. No longer are we locked into old English, needing someone to "translate" and interpret for us the archaic words. God has raised up hundreds of modern-day "Levites" over the last several years—men and women who thoroughly know Old Testament Hebrew and New Testament Greek, and who have given to us translations that are both literal and contemporary. We can walk into thousands of bookstores everywhere and buy Bibles translated into modern English.

Most Christians, however, do not study the Bible regularly on their own, partly because we simply neglect this unique opportunity and responsibility. There's another reason, however. Many Christians do not know *how* to study the Bible regularly. They have no method. And study suggestions that are often presented are too complicated and difficult to use.

Following is a simple plan to help you to study the Scriptures regularly, perferably on a daily basis. But before we look at the specific plan, there are several preliminary steps you need to take:

1. Determine you're going to study the Bible regularly.

2. Decide on a study time that fits best into your own personal schedule (early morning is best, but not always possible).

3. Choose the *place* that you can use regularly.

4. Secure a good literal, but modern translation (we suggest the *New International Version* or the *New American Standard Bible*). You may also wish to secure one or two other translations to use for comparative study.

5. Use a study guide that: (a.) is simple enough to be practical for you, (b.) is flexible enough to fit into your schedule, and (c.) helps you *read, interpret* and *apply* the Scriptures.

6. Purchase a notebook in which you can record the results of your study.

7. Select and purchase a quality hymnbook you can use for meditation, worship and praise.

Life Response

Figure 5 presents a specific plan for personal Bible study. It is one that we developed for our own people to use at Fellowship Bible Church in Dallas, Texas. Each week, on a special message outline, we give the people six Bible passages for daily study which will prepare them for the forthcoming message next weekend. In addition we provide them with copies of this Personal Bible Study Guide.[1]

The guide is quite self-explanatory.[1] There is a place to record the passage, a title for the study (to be determined after the study is complete) and a date. The eight steps are also quite clear.

Step 1.—PRAY. *Praise God and ask Him through the Holy Spirit to illuminate your mind.* Praising and thanking God for who He is and what He has done is a good way to prepare your heart for personal Bible study. A very effective way to do this is to read the words of both the great old hymns of the faith as well as contemporary hymns. For example, "Great Is Thy Faithfulness," or "How Great Thou Art" are excellent illustrations of hymns that focus on God's character. So is "Holy Holy Holy."

This is why I suggest that you secure a good hymnal. I personally like to use *Hymns for the Family of God,* produced by Paragon Associates, Inc., Nashville, Tennessee. However, any good hymnal will do.

NOTE: Try singing some of the hymns (you may wish to make sure you're alone). And don't worry about your voice quality. Make a joyful sound to the Lord even if you have difficulty "making music." God will enjoy it.

Personal Bible Study Guide

Passage: Phillipians 1:1-6 Title: _____ Date: _____

1. Pray . . .
2. Survey . . .
3. Read . . .
4. Observe . . .

5. Interpret . . .
6. Apply . . .
7. Pray . . .
8. Share . . .

READING AND RECORDING

What does the Bible say? Copy key statements and verses for the passage.

"i thank my God... remembrance of you." v3

"i am confident... He will perfect it." v6

INTERPRETING AND UNDERSTANDING

What do these statements mean? Put in your own words (outline, ask questions, etc.).

He had pleasant memories of them. Why? See Acts 16 for clues.

He prayed for them regularly.

APPLYING AND OBEYING

How do these statements apply to my life?
What will I do?

What Christians do i remember this way and pray for?

Here are some for today:

Harold Garner
Dick Mohline
Don Logue

When will I do it?

Immediately

With whom will I do it?

Alone this morning — with wife this evening.

Step 2—SURVEY. *Read the passage quickly.* It is important to get an overview of the passage of Scripture before studying it in detail. Do what step 2 says—read the passage *quickly*. Don't concentrate on details. Look at the forest first. Your next step will be to go back and study the individual trees.

Step 3—READ. *Read the passage carefully.*

Step 4—OBSERVE. *Look for biblical statements that are especially meaningful. Copy these statements in column 1.* Steps 3 and 4 should be taken together. As you read carefully, look for those statements that are particularly meaningful to you. How many statements you write in the first column entitled "Reading and Recording" depends on the time you have for personal study and also the nature of the passage. You may decide to copy only one significant statement.

Step 5—INTERPRET. *Record in column 2 what those biblical statements mean. Note: Be sure to consider the larger context.* Interpretation is a very important process. Note that you are not concentrating on application, but rather on what the Bible is actually teaching in a literal, historical setting. You may outline what it means and, you may actually ask questions about what it means. Don't be concerned if you don't understand completely.

Step 6—APPLY. *Record in column 3 what you can do to apply these statements in your life.* Application is the most difficult phase in personal Bible study. It is very easy and convenient to stop with OBSERVE and INTERPRET. But, to really benefit from your study you must think about how the biblical statements you have copied on your sheet apply to your life personally. It will help you to answer the question "What will I do?" as a result of this study. It will also help you to answer the questions "*When* will I do it?" and "With *whom* will I do it?"

NOTE: It is not always possible to answer these questions in great detail. In some instances, when you answer the question, "With whom will I do it?" you will simply respond that it will involve your relationship with God.

Remember, too, that sometimes applications are cumulative. If you are studying related passages over several days, you may discover that you will be led to a culminating application as a result of several days of study. In other words, don't be frustrated if you have difficulty applying every single statement.

Step 7—PRAY. *Use your observations and applications as a basis for prayer and praise.* Many times we have difficulty talking to God in a meaningful way. Your personal Bible studies will help you to have something to say to the Lord on a regular basis. Your three columns will provide you with a prayer outline. Use what you have written as a basis for your communication with the Lord. And, of course, when you come to column 3, you can specifically ask Him to help you to apply to your own life what the Holy Spirit has taught you.

Step 8—SHARE. *Look for a natural opportunity to encourage someone with what you have learned.* This is not always possible. The important word is "natural." If you ask God to provide you with those opportunities, you will be surprised at how they come along. And when they are "natural," you will not feel as if you are demonstrating a "super spiritual" attitude that could be misinterpreted.

Note
1. Adapted from a Bible Study Guide developed by Chuck Miller of BARNABAS, Inc., an organization that specializes in Discipling Ministries Seminars. Box 218, Highland, California 92346. Used by permission.

12

Nehemiah's
Toughest Task

Nehemiah 13:4-31

Following Ezra's special teaching ministry in Israel, Nehemiah's next major effort involved the repopulating of Jerusalem (see Neh. 11:1—12:26). And at some point in the total process just described they dedicated the wall of Jerusalem with a great service of singing and praise to God (see 12:27-47).

Other than these major events following the rebuilding of the wall, we are not told specifically what transpired step by step in Nehemiah's life for the 12 years he served on the scene as governor in Judah. In fact, he makes very little reference to himself in chapters 7 to 12. However, we can conclude it was a very successful period of time in the life of Israel.

At the end of this 12-year period, Nehemiah returned to Susa, evidently to once again serve King Artaxerxes.

How long he remained in this position, we do not know. However, we can speculate that it involved a rather lengthy period of time, for while he was gone some rather startling changes took place in Judah that were serious violations of Israel's written covenant with God. When Nehemiah once again returned to Judah, he found a task that in some respects must have been even more difficult for him to face than rebuilding the wall. That's why I've entitled this final chapter "Nehemiah's Toughest Task"!

His Encounter with Tobiah (Neh. 13:4-9)

The name Tobiah was not new in Nehemiah's narrative. He was one of Nehemiah's archenemies. who, along with Sanballat and several others, had consistently tried to stop the building of the wall 12 years earlier. During that time we'd been involved in a conspiracy to militarily attack the children of Israel. He'd also been part of the diabolical scheme to harm Nehemiah—perhaps even to assassinate him. When these efforts failed, he did everything else he could to discredit Nehemiah, including writing numerous letters to those in Jerusalem who were sympathetic to his cause, as well as to Nehemiah personally (see 6:17-19).

When Nehemiah returned to Jerusalem he was shocked to find that Eliashib, the high priest in Israel, had prepared a special guest room for Tobiah in the temple. What made it even more shocking, the large chamber the high priest had prepared for Tobiah included several rooms where the tithes and offering of the people were to be stored so that the priestly ministry could continue in Israel as God had outlined in His law. Furthermore, this was also the room where the various utensils and frankincense were stored which the priest used in offering sacrifices to the Lord.

Needless to say, Nehemiah was *very* distressed! After all Tobiah had done to try to hinder God's work in Israel, it was hard to believe what had happened. Nehemiah was so angry—and understandably so—that he went into the temple and literally "threw all of Tobiah's household goods out of the room" (13:8). He then "gave an order" for the rooms to be cleansed (13:9). It appears that Nehemiah wanted every trace of Tobiah's presence removed from the temple. To put it bluntly, he had the room fumigated!

His Encounter with the
Officials in Israel (Neh. 13:10-14).

Nehemiah's next task relates to why Tobiah was able to have a guest room in the temple. The children of Israel had failed in their commitment to pay their tithes and offerings. The room Tobiah occupied—which was to be the "storehouse" for the gifts of the people—was empty and unused. Consequently, the Levites and the others who were to live off of these offerings as they performed spiritual services for the people had to go back to their regular jobs (see 13:10).

Nehemiah reprimanded the officials in Israel for neglecting their responsibility to make sure the children of Israel obeyed the Lord in these matters. What made these events even more distressing for Nehemiah, and difficult to believe, is that these leaders in Israel had previously signed a document, promising before the Lord and the people that they would never again let this happen in Israel (see 10:32-39).

Nehemiah, in his inimitable style, then proceeded to correct the situation. In his own words, he recorded, "Then I gathered them [the Levites] together and restored them to their posts. All Judah then brought the tithe of the grain, wine, and oil into the storehouses (13:11,12).

His Encounter with Those Who Were Profaning the
Sabbath (Neh. 13:15-22)

Another commitment Israel had made in writing was

to not break God's laws regarding the Sabbath day (see 10:31). However, when Nehemiah returned to Jerusalem he found they had also violated this promise. He discovered "some who were treading wine presses on the sabbath, and bringing in sacks of grain and loading them on donkeys, as well as wine, grapes, figs, and all kinds of loads, and they brought them into Jerusalem on the sabbath day" (13:15).

In addition, there were men of Tyre who actually moved into Jerusalem and set up their own businesses. The leaders in Israel were allowing them to operate their shops on the Sabbath day (see 13:16).

Like the other problems, Nehemiah faced this one head-on. He "reprimanded the nobles of Judah and said to them, 'What is this evil thing you are doing, by profaning the sabbath day' " (13:17).

He then asked them a very pointed question: "Did not your fathers do the same so that our God brought on us, and on this city, all this trouble? Yet you are adding to the wrath on Israel by profaning the sabbath" (13:18).

Nehemiah no doubt found it hard to believe that Israel so quickly had regressed to *their* own sinful ways. How quickly memories fade when blessings are restored and problems cease. How soon "foxhole prayers" are forgotten.

His Encounter with Those Who Violated Their Marriage Commitments (Neh. 13:23-31)

Once Nehemiah cleansed the temple of Tobiah's presence, reestablished God's plan for the people and the priesthood, and restored the Sabbath, he yet faced his most difficult confrontation. The children of Israel had also promised in writing that they would not intermarry with pagan people—those who did not worship and serve the one true God (see 10:30). And yet when Nehemiah arrived back in Jerusalem, he found they had violated this commitment as well. Some of the Jews "had married women from Ashdod, Ammon, and Moab" (13:23).

This incredible phenomenon in Israel frustrated Nehemiah more than all their other sins. His actions were probably unprecedented in his leadership in Israel. He was so disturbed and angry with those who had committed this sin that he "contended with them and cursed them" (v. 25), that is, he pronounced God's judgment upon them. The depth of his disappointment and the intensity of his anger is seen in that he "struck some of them and pulled out their hair, and made them swear by God, 'You shall not give your daughters to their sons, nor take of their daughters for your sons or for yourselves' " (13:25).

Out of context this may seem like violent and inappropriate behavior for a man of God. However, when interpreted against the backdrop of Israel's long-range as well as immediate history, we can readily understand Nehemiah's extreme behavior. This very sin was at the heart of why they were taken into Babylonian captivity in the first place. And this is why he reminded them of a very important historical fact: "Did not Solomon king of Israel sin regarding these things?" he asked as he unleashed his righteous fury. "Yet among the many nations there was no king like him, and he was loved by his God, and God made him king over all Israel; nevertheless the *foreign woman* caused even him to sin" (13:26).

The implication is clear. Nehemiah was concerned about God's judgment which could again fall on Israel; he had seen and experienced it before. And he knew God would never tolerate this sin. If He had not allowed it in Solomon's life and had judged all Israel because of it, Nehemiah knew in his heart He would not allow it now.

Nehemiah's concern then was for Israel as a whole. And no doubt his frustration was accentuated because of his own personal involvement. After all, he had sacrificed Israel. And even laid his own life on the line.

But in looking back over Nehemiah's total life as we've viewed it in this historical narrative, I personally would have to conclude that his disappointment and anger at this moment was not nearly so much related to his feelings of being let down and taken for granted. Rather, he was more concerned about what this would mean to others in Israel who were attempting to obey God's laws. And above all, I firmly believe he was motivated by the same feelings that Jesus felt when He cleansed the temple. In that situation, Christ "made a scourge of cords, and drove them [the money changers] all out of the temple, with the sheep and the oxen; and He poured out the coins of the money-changers, and overturned their tables" (John 2:15).

Then after this rather violent behavior on the part of Jesus Christ, the disciples remembered that it had been written of Jesus in the Old Testament, "Zeal for Thy house will consume me" (John 2:17).

I believe this was also Nehemiah's primary motivation. Though he was certainly concerned with his own personal standing before God, which is obvious from his three prayers in the final chapter (see 13:14,22,31), he was primarily concerned that God's will be done in Israel.

Lessons for Twentieth-Century Christians

Nehemiah's attitudes and actions in this final chapter of this Old Testament book that bears his name leave us with what we might also identify as the most difficult task for responsible Christians: responsibility for admonishing and confronting other Christians who are violating the will of God.

The New Testament clearly outlines how confrontation is to be done. However, church discipline is a subject in itself and space prohibits me from dealing with it in this chapter. Rather, I've chosen to concentrate on what we can learn from the specific problems Nehemiah faced.

Let's look at these problems from a New Testament perspective. There are at least three.

1. Failure to honor God in our associations. This involves allowing non-Christians to influence our lives negatively. It is illustrated by both Tobiah's presence in the temple as well as by those who intermarried with the pagan people in the land of Israel. And this principle is reiterated by Paul in the New Testament in his second letter to the Corinthians. His instructions are specific and to the point: "Do not be bound together with unbelievers; for what partnership have righteousness and lawlessness, or what fellowship has light with darkness? Or what harmony has Christ with Belial, or what has a believer in common with an unbeliever? Or what agreement has the temple of God with idols? For we are the temple of the living God" (2 Cor. 6:14-16).

Then to show the relationship between what God expected from the children of Israel in Old Testament days and what He expects from Christians, Paul quotes a series of Old Testament passages to get his point across: "For we are the temple of the living God; just as God said, 'I will dwell in them and walk among them; and I will be their God, and they shall be My people. Therefore, come out from their midst and be separate, says the Lord. And do not touch what is unclean; and I will welcome you. And I will be a father to you. And you shall be sons and daughters to Me, says the Lord Almighty' " (2 Cor. 6:16-18).

Obviously, this does not mean we must set ourselves apart totally from non-Christians. Separation does not mean isolation. And Paul dealt with this very practical issue in his first letter to the Corinthians. In an earlier letter he had instructed them "not to associate with immoral people"—meaning a "so-called *brother* if he should be an immoral person, or covetous, or an idolater, or a reviler, or a drunkard, or a swindler" (1 Cor. 5:9,11). Some of the

Corinthians misunderstood Paul and thought he was saying they should not associate at all with non-Christians who are living this kind of life. Paul quickly clarified this point by saying, "I did not at all mean with the immoral people of this world, or with the covetous and swindlers, or with idolaters; for then you would have to go out of the world" (1 Cor. 5:10).

Paul here recognizes of course that it is impossible to live in this world without associating with non-Christians. However, to associate with them is one thing; to allow them to influence our lives negatively is another. And this is what we must constantly be on guard against, without taking our Christian influence away from them.

The most obvious and specific lesson that comes from this story in the book of Nehemiah as well as from the New Testament setting in Corinth is that if a Christian marries someone who does not share his or her faith, the Christian is asking for serious trouble. Such a marriage is a violation of God's perfect will. It is true that in some instances it works out. Sometimes the unsaved partner becomes a Christian. At other times, the person may not be a Christian but he/she is tolerant of the mate's faith in Christ. In some rare instances the non-Christian partner may even support the spouse in the faith. However, in more instances than not, marriages of this sort lead to disappointment and heartbreak and often separation and divorce. We cannot deliberately walk out of the will of God and expect God's blessing upon us.

Another area of application is in our business associations. For example, I knew a Christian businessman who went into partnership with a non-Christian whose value system was out of harmony with Christian principles. Both men were at a partnership-management level. This kind of "marriage" was devastating and a "divorce" was inevitable—creating a great deal of heartache and emotional pain for everyone involved.

*2. Failure to honor God with our material posses-
sions.* God established certain laws in Israel regarding
tithing. His people were to give one-tenth of all of their
material resources to meet the physical needs of the Levites. When Nehemiah returned from Susa, the children of
Israel were not being obedient in this area of their lives.
Consequently, the Levites were not able to minister to the
people spiritually, which added yet further to the moral
and spiritual breakdown in Israel.

"Tithing" per se is not reiterated in the New Testament. In fact, it is true that Israel set aside more than 10
percent for the Lord's work. In addition to the 10 percent
set aside for the Levites, they were to set aside 10 percent
for a special celebration in Jerusalem (see Deut.
12:5,6,11,18).

Furthermore, every *third* year an additional 10 percent
was collected to care for strangers, the fatherless, widows,
and any additional needs the Levites might have (Deut.
14:28,29). In other words, the children of Israel were to
give approximately 23 percent of their resources each year
to carry on the work of God.

Even so, God introduces, in the New Testament, principles of giving that rise above the law. Paul outlines these
principles in his Corinthian letters.

● We are to give *systematically.* In writing to the Corinthians Paul instructed them to set aside a sum of money
"on the first day of every week" (1 Cor. 16:2). Obviously,
there were cultural factors involved in this pattern, but the
principle is clear. Though Christians in our culture may be
paid every two weeks, or monthly, or even in some instances yearly, they are to set aside a certain amount
regularly to give to God's work. Christians are to give
systematically. It is not to be haphazard. It is to be planned
just as carefully as any other item in our budgets.

● We are to give *proportionately.* In the same verse Paul
instructed the Corinthians that each person should give "in

keeping with his income" *(NIV)*. If he made much, he was to give much; if he did not make much, he was to give less. But they were *all* to give, no matter how small or large their income.

● We are to give *cheerfully*. In Paul's second letter to the Corinthians he laid down a third principle: "Remember this: Whoever sows sparingly will also reap sparingly, and whoever sows generously will also reap generously. Each man should give what he has decided in his heart to give, not reluctantly or under compulsion, for God loves a *cheerful* giver" (2 Cor. 9:6,7, *NIV*).

God is not pleased if we give reluctantly and under compulsion. This is the principle of grace. Freely we have received and freely we are to give. This is true worship. And this is true gratitude for what God has given to us in Jesus Christ.

● When we give according to God's principle *we can expect God to meet our needs*. Following Paul's instructions to give generously and cheerfully he also wrote: "God is able to make all grace abound to you, so that in all things at all times, having all that you need, you will abound in every good work" (2 Cor. 9:8, *NIV*).

It's important to note that God has not promised to multiply our income if we give. But He has promised to meet our needs. And if we give out of a heart of love, there are very few instances when God does not pour out unusual blessings on Christians—both financially and spiritually.

How much then should a Christian give? The Bible doesn't say specifically. Rather, we are to give *systematically, proportionately,* and *cheerfully* expecting that we cannot outgive God. He will not let us down, though He may test our motives to help us truly give out of a heart of love. When Christians give according to these principles, there will be plenty of money to support God's work. Indeed, just as in the Old Tetament, we are under obligation to take care of those particularly who labor in the gospel (see Matt. 10:10; Luke 10:7; 1 Tim. 5:17,18; 1 Cor. 9:7-23).

What indeed are the facts? Some studies show that the average Christian gives as little as one or two percent of his material possessions to the Lord's work. It appears that because Christians are under grace and not under law, as in the Old Testament, we simply take advantage of God's grace. The more He gives, the more we tend to keep as our own, not realizing that it *all* belongs to Him.

There is yet another reason for poor response in giving. Nehemiah had to confront the leaders in Israel because they had not taught the people properly. As I have studied this passage, the Lord brought me under conviction, for often I shy away from this important Old Testament and New Testament concept. To avoid teaching this principle is to violate the will of God and to cause others to do the same. I think God is saying the same thing to every spiritual leader in the church who is entrusted with pastoral teaching responsibilities.

One final thought! If Israel under law was to give 10 percent so the Levites could carry out the work of God, it seems that this ought to be a good *starting point* for Christians who are living under grace. I've been extremely impressed as I have read the stories of Christians who have struggled with the concept of tithing, and then have made that decision—not out of obligation, but out of love for Christ. The end result is exciting.

One story that has intrigued me is that told by Mary Crowley. Her early years were spent as an orphan. In her quest for security and hope, her first marriage ended in divorce. She was left with two children and full responsibility in the depression years.

Her income was so meager she could hardly pay her bills. "There was just no way that I could tithe," she concluded. As she sat at her kitchen table after the children were asleep one evening, she figured up her stack of bills, her budget for groceries, her rent, her housekeeping expenses, her bus fare for going to work and church. "If I added 10 percent of my salary to the debit side of my budget," she thought, "there would be nothing at all left in the miscellaneous column—no money for Christmas presents, books for the kids, or the dentist."[1]

But the more Mary prayed, the more she was impressed that she should set aside 10 percent of her income for her church, not out of obligation but because she wanted to honor God. The story that unfolds in her life is incredible. Today Mary Crowley operates a multi-million-dollar enterprise called Home Interiors and Gifts, Inc., located in Dallas, Texas. In 1976 her annual sales were over one hundred million dollars. And each year she gives multiplied thousands of dollars to God's work. She is perhaps one of the most benevolent Christians living today.

Will God do this for every Christian who is faithful in giving? Not at all! The facts are that Mary Crowley became what she is because of a lot of hard work, motivation, and prayer. But intricately blended with that work and prayer is the fact that she was faithful to the Lord with her money. And the more He blessed her, the more she gave. I'm convinced that God does honor the application of that principle in our lives.

3. Failure to honor God with our time (Heb. 10:24,25). In the Old Testament God established the Sabbath as a day of rest for Israel. It was a rigid law and was not to be violated in any way. In the New Testament, God does not place us under this strict system. Rather, every day is to be a special day for God.

But just as Christians take advantage of God's grace once they have been released from a strict law of giving, we also take advantage of God's grace once released from a strict Sabbath law. How easy to neglect our time spent in service for God, with other Christians, and with our families. The author of the Hebrew letter speaks to this issue pointedly: "Let us consider how to stimulate one another to love and good deeds, *not forsaking our own assembling together,* as is the habit of some but encouraging one another; and *all the more,* as you see the day drawing near" (Heb. 10:24,25).

There is yet another dimension to this principle. Some Christians never take a day of rest and, in not doing so, they abuse their own bodies, which the Bible calls the "temple of God." To neglect our day of rest, it seems, is to violate not a law of God per se, that is written for unqualified obedience, but rather a psychological and physical law which is reflected in the specific religious law in the Old Testament.

I remember hearing the story one day of two men who were taking a trip across the great northland. Each had a dog team. One man decided to drive his dogs day after day without giving them one day in seven to rest. The other man decided to stop the seventh day and to rest his team.

Weeks passed in this long journey. As the story goes, by the time these men reached the destination, the man who rested his dogs every seventh day reached the destination point far ahead of the man who drove his team week after week without that day to recuperate and rest.

Is there inherent in God's Old Testament law a principle that goes beyond the spiritual? I think there is, and Christians who violate it are not only spending time for themselves they should be spending time with God, but they're also doing themselves a disservice in interfering with their ultimate effectiveness as a Christian.

Life Response

Think carefully about the following questions:

1. Am I honoring God with my associations? Am I

allowing non-Christians to drag me down spiritually? Am I allowing them to cause me to do things out of the will of God?

Action step (if applicable): _____

2. Do I honor God with my material possessions? What percentage of my material resources am I giving to God? Am I giving proportionately as God has blessed me? Am I faithful in meeting the physical needs of those who minister to me?

Action step (if applicable): _____

3. Do I honor God with my time? How do I spend the Lord's day? Am I negligent in spending time encouraging and building up other Christians? What about my own personal program for rest and relaxation? Am I honoring God with my total being—body, mind and soul?

Action step (if applicable): _____

Note
1. Mary C. Crowley, *Think Mink* (Old Tappan, NJ: Fleming H. Revell Company, 1976), p. 33.

THE BIBLICAL RENEWAL SERIES
by
Gene A. Getz

ONE ANOTHER SERIES

Building Up One Another
Encouraging One Another
Loving One Another
Praying for One Another
Serving One Another

THE MEASURE OF SERIES

Measure of a . . .
  Church
  Family
  Man
  Marriage
  Woman

PERSONALITY SERIES

When You're Confused and Uncertain (Abraham)
When You Feel Rejected (Joseph)
When Your Goals Seem Out of Reach (Nehemiah)
When the Job Seems Too Big (Joshua)
When You Feel Like a Failure (David)
When the Pressure's On (Elijah)
When You Feel You Haven't Got It (Moses)

BIBLE BOOK SERIES

Pressing on When You'd Rather Turn Back
(Philippians)
Saying No When You'd Rather Say Yes
(Titus)
Believing God When You Are Tempted to Doubt
(James 1)
Doing Your Part When You'd Rather Let God Do It All (James
2-5)
Looking Up When You Feel Down
(Ephesians 1-3)
Living for Others When You'd Rather Live for Yourself
(Ephesians 4-6)
Standing Firm When You'd Rather Retreat
(1 Thessalonians)